ANOTHER TIME, ANOTHER PLACE

ANOTHER TIME, ANOTHER PLACE

MARGARITA LUDOVIC

AuthorHouse™
1663 Liberty Drive
Bloomington, IN 47403
www.authorhouse.com
Phone: 1-800-839-8640

© 2012 by Margarita Ludovic. All rights reserved.

No part of this book may be reproduced, stored in a retrieval system, or transmitted by any means without the written permission of the author.

Published by AuthorHouse   10/31/2012

ISBN: 978-1-4772-4213-1 (sc)
ISBN: 978-1-4772-4214-8 (hc)
ISBN: 978-1-4772-4215-5 (e)

Any people depicted in stock imagery provided by Thinkstock are models, and such images are being used for illustrative purposes only.
Certain stock imagery © Thinkstock.

Because of the dynamic nature of the Internet, any web addresses or links contained in this book may have changed since publication and may no longer be valid. The views expressed in this work are solely those of the author and do not necessarily reflect the views of the publisher, and the publisher hereby disclaims any responsibility for them.

For my children – my best friends,

and all my lovely grandchildren

Preface

> All the world's a stage,
> And all the men and women merely players:
> They have their exits and their entrances;
> And one man in his time plays many parts,
> (Shakespeare)

Looking back over my early beginnings, I played many parts, succeeded in some and failed dismally in others.

How come I was not afraid of facing a firing squad or being interrogated by Czech or Russian military police?

I suppose that children do not think of the consequences but bravely face the immediate situation.

2.

Although desperate to be loved and feel wanted I was not afraid to speak up when others needed my help, young that I was.

How did my early childhood experiences affect my life? Well this feeling of needing love and the need to be needed stayed with me, so that I often made myself into a 'door mat' so that others would not think badly of me.

I cannot blame my past history. We are what we make of ourselves, and should take responsibility for our actions, however wrong, or indeed right. Oh I still have my dreams and a passion for living, excitement, adventure, a need to achieve and of course to be truly and unquestionably loved.

To the outside world I achieved fantastic family life, managed to climb the professional ladder with honour and led a very busy and interesting life. I was an entrepreneur in every way and always wanted the best for all my family, and like a tigress, would fight to achieve that.

Looking back, I had to climb one mountain after another and still had a long way to go. Intrepidly I built up the family unit, was respected as an Educationalist and enjoyed leading a creative Arts Council.

The big world beckoned and I travelled far and wide through Europe, Israel, Egypt, Peru, Ecuador, Galapagos Islands, Thailand, China, Japan, Russia, India and Africa, first with my husband and latterly on my own, joining various small adventurous groups.

Then everything seemed to collapse about me and I found myself alone.

Oh to be a fearless, little girl again and re-build my future, such as it is.

Introduction

There were no fanfares, no trumpets or the sounds of a heavenly choir welcoming this baby. It was just a normal, dark, wet and stormy November night, with the wind howling in from the Adriatic Sea and the rain beating a tattoo against the window pane. A young, frightened woman lay in a dingy bedroom in the throws of labour. Far from home, family and friends she had little advice or comfort for what lay ahead. An old crone of a midwife was in attendance, speaking only Italian, for this was taking place in Trieste—Italy.

This young woman was my about-to-be mother. She was not looking forward to the birth of her first baby, as it was unwanted by her, being only a young woman on the threshold of a sparkling stage career and a baby would only be a hindrance to her. She had tried hard to abort the foetus but no doctor would help her get rid of the unwanted pregnancy, as that was illegal. Thus she found herself in this sad predicament, having a baby in a strange country, without money or the back up of a health authority or welfare state. Being of German nationality, she was a foreigner in Italy and therefore had to fend for herself.

She was left on her own in the bedroom and the would-be father was kept well away from her. Being on her own for what seemed an eternity, and not quite knowing what was about to pass, she was terrified, as her upbringing by nuns had not prepared her for this ordeal, and neither had her mother, who was far away in Germany. When the pains became so bad that she could hardly move, she threw her shoes against the bedroom

Margarita Ludovic

door, in order to attract some attention. The old midwife appeared, and what seemed like days later, the angry cries of the newborn baby were heard and the proud father, who was very pleased with the event of having an offspring, rushed into the room.

Thus I made my dramatic entrance into a world about to be torn apart by Hitler's rise, but let me start at the beginning.

Ludwig Bendiner, then in his forties was my father and came from a Jewish family.

One of his brothers was uncle Wilhelm, a lovely man and I have vague memories of him. He adored me and always made a great fuss of me. He never married, but stayed close to my father, working by his side, building up a theatrical Bendiner empire. I know next to nothing about the rest of my father's family, except that they were all connected to the theatre and film world, and were a close-knit family. Partly they lived in Berlin and Hamburg, where they were well known, or they went on tour all around Europe. Wilhelm and my father worked together in their own production company and touring theatre and Resi, a niece, often joined the company as a singer.

By the time I was old enough to ask questions about my Bendiner family, Wilhelm, Joseph, Mathilda and Emma were dead in some concentration camp, while Max, an old man by then had returned to Hamburg and died there. Resi was in England and I was destined to join her there at a later date after the war. But more of that later.

My father, Ludwig was born in Graz, Austria on the 27th June 1879. He was a very handsome and charming and loved the attention of women, who absolutely adored him. He had ex lovers all over Europe and I was told he even sired a son to a lady in New York while travelling around and working in the States although I have never been able to trace this half brother of mine.

Whenever on tour, my father had plenty of invites from ladies who found him fascinating and fell in love with him. They all wanted to be his sponsors and invited him to stay in their apartments.

During the First World War he found himself in Istanbul—having joined the Vienna Operetten Theatre as stage director. Later he worked in Vienna, Prague and Berlin. Sometime during his early life, he somehow became a Czech citizen due to the break-up of the Austrian/Hungarian Empire—so I was told—but he never spoke a single word of Czech and remained an Austrian at heart, speaking only German.

Next my father went to live in Germany, Berlin, where he produced various shows, both musicals, vaudeville and straight plays, as well as some films. Being musically talented, he was asked to work for the Performing Rights Society, attending various concerts, in order to check that the proposed works were indeed being performed, and performing rights had been paid and granted. He only had to hear a few bars of each piece to know what was being played. His musical repertoire was immense.

Handsome, talented and already successful, he then created his own theatre company continuing to produce light operas and vaudeville with many young talented actors and singers, acrobats and a team of 'Lilliputaners' (dwarfs) of whom he was particularly fond. The company was resident in Berlin and Hamburg where the Bendiner family was already well known, but he also continued the family tradition of touring around Europe, often working with his brother Wilhelm.

Thus it came to pass that my father was on tour with the company, visiting the town of Bayreuth, Bavaria—home of Richard Wagner, where he first met my mother, Anita.

Anita Pajak was born 3rd of August 1913 and was the youngest daughter born to Franciska and Michael Pajak, a catholic family, living at the time in Weiden, Bavaria.

There were five children in that family. I only really knew my mother's two sisters, as the girls were very close. The eldest sister, was my aunt Emma, or Emmi as we called her, and next came Agnes, called Agi, who was inseparable from my mother. Then there were two brothers. My grandmother, (mother to my mother) was a great lady, and was one of ten children.

Anna, the youngest of the ten, my great aunt, was the only one I knew on my grandmother's side; She married the wealthy Haase and owned several privately owned cinemas. It was she who was responsible for delving into our family history resulting in finding that the family could be traced back as far as the eleventh century, and that it was linked to a noble home in Sweden. Our coat of arms was a lynx.

My mother never knew her father, as he had been drafted into the army during the First World War and shortly afterwards died under an avalanche in Austria, while serving his country. Which country, you may ask, as he was born a German—a Bavarian, but had to take on Polish nationality when borders changed during the frequent re-shuffles. Thus, at the time of her birth, my mother was in fact Polish, and became German at a later date.

Times were very hard for the widowed mother, (my grandmother), who had to raise her five children alone. However, when she herself had been a young girl, she had been put into service in wealthy Austrian house and had learnt to put her hand to everything. She learnt how to cook and soon earned herself a good reputation and was often invited to help out at various functions. Thus she tried catering as well working in a factory or as a field hand—she would turn her hand to any job to keep the wolf from the door.

Being of a good catholic family, the church helped out by taking the three girls into care. All three girls were boarded in a children's home that was an orphanage and was attached to the church in Weiden, Bavaria, where they all lived at that time. The boys were sent elsewhere. My mother was only four then and life was very hard for all the young sisters. Living in the orphanage they knew little of comfort. Life was spartan and there was no time for childhood games, toys, freedom or enjoyment of any sort. They had to join the religious life and sang in all the church services—even the baby, my mother, who had a beautiful, clear voice. They were lucky to receive a good basic education from the nuns—simple but thorough.

When my mother was about eight, the family moved to Regensburg where the girls helped to boost the family income by collecting slops from various restaurants, and selling it on to the pig farmers. Their stay in

Regensburg was short-lived and once again the family moved on to Bayreuth, where my grandmother's wealthy sister Anna Haase lived.

The girls attended school until they were fourteen, thirteen and twelve years old (respectively), and then went to a factory to work. They also worked for a jewelry company by painting pretty broaches at home as piece work. In the evening they went to work for their aunt Haase, who owned the big, luxury cinema in Bayreuth, which also doubled as a theatre when touring companies came to town. The girls helped with the sale of tickets, looked after clients' outer garments during the performances and helped with the cleaning after the shows—all under the eagle eye of their mother, my grandmother.

Life was hard but the girls made their own fun and as they got older went out dancing and enjoyed themselves as and when they could, as they were all very attractive young women. They were always referred to as the 'Three Graces'

One day the cinema announced the forthcoming production of a Variety show that was touring Germany at the time. This caused great excitement. Everything was made ready to receive the touring company and anticipation was at fever pitch. The girls all had to help and my mother was a most willing helper as her imagination was fired by this event. She was not let down in any way. Having sneaked in to watch every performance, she was ready to forsake everything in order to join the company. She walked on air and dreamt of a glittering future in the theatre. Plucking up every ounce of courage, she approached the director of the company—Mr Ludwig Bendiner and begged him to take her with him and let her join the company. She was untrained, and not yet sixteen. Mr Bendiner, (my father to be), having an eye for a pretty girl, saw her potential, but told her that he had no vacancy at present. Anyway she was still under age and would have to wait a little while longer. He promised he would send for her as soon as a vacancy occurred.

Undaunted, my mother continued to watch every show and tried to remember dances and songs to practice at home. But too soon the company left; leaving my mother living in hope that one day soon Mr Bendiner would remember and send for her.

Time passed and before her seventeenth birthday, Mr Bendiner was true to his word and sent a telegram for her to come and join the company in Hamburg. Oh, my mother was so excited and could hardly await her departure. Her mother, my grandmother was against the whole venture and had great misgivings, but times were hard and if my mother could make something of herself it would be all to the good, as such opportunities were far and few. In great haste my mother made ready to leave and with her mother's parting words 'don't you dare come home with a Jew-child', echoing in her head, left home.

Having arrived safely in Hamburg, she quickly settled into theatre life and, as she was intelligent, quick witted as well as very beautiful, soon made her mark as an invaluable member of the cast. Life was great and my mother enjoyed every moment of it.

She quickly progressed into the front line of the chorus as she proved to be a talented dancer and singer. Catching the eye of the film directors, she also often walked away with small parts in plays and films, making the leading ladies very jealous.

My father adored her and promoted her at every possible occasion and took her with him where ever he went. They set up home together in Hamburg and in Berlin, near the Bendiner family. My parents had a beautiful flat, just below the world famous tenor, Richard Tauber. They were well acquainted and sometimes worked together.

My mother enjoyed all the attention she was receiving for the first time in her life. She loved visiting the Berlin Opera where the Bendiners always had their own box at their disposal. Life was good and who would have thought the little waif from the children's home would be such a success. It was an exciting, scintillating life for the young woman, who was adored by everyone.

Alas Hitler's rise to power had been fast and he was well on the way to have the power of cleansing the German Nation of any impurities, wanting only a true Arian race. Wherever Jews lived, he wanted them to be persecuted. A campaign of terror was started against the Jews—books were burnt, shops demolished, rights of citizenship were stripped. All those who could, fled Germany, as did some of the Bendiner family.

My father, having read the writing on the wall at an early stage, had already taken my mother to Austria, but this was not really a safe place. They had lost all their possessions and travelled lightly, with only a suitcase. To my mother's horror, she found that she was expecting a baby, which did not help the situation. She could hardly seek help from her family in Bavaria, who had threatened her not to come home with a Jew child. She went to see various doctors, but as abortions were illegal, she had to keep the baby, very much against her will. After her quick rise to fame and fortune, this was a sad come down and although she continued her stage career wherever she could, life was over shadowed by the dark, political clouds that were spreading over Europe.

My parents had to flee yet again, and went to Czechoslovakia where one of my father's former mistresses helped them to travel to Italy, where yet another kind lady helped them financially so that they could find accommodation. They found a very small, inexpensive flat and my father tried to find work, lending his hand to any job that was offered. My mother found work in cabaret and danced every night, while she could, before people noticed that she was with child. She loved the stage and resented my eminent arrival. No way did she want to be lumbered with a baby. My father on the other hand could hardly await the joyful event.

Now looking back at my parent's upbringing, education and experiences of life, I wonder how it all affected me in later life. Anyway, for better or for worse, the scene was set for my howling entry into the world on that wet, dark November night.

Chapter 1

I was a fat baby, resembling one of those puppies whose skin hangs in rolls and wrinkles around its body. However, my father adored me and chose the name Daisy for me, after his favourite character in the operetta *The Dollar Princess*. He used to have a boxer dog he had also named Daisy, who had died, and now there I was, probably reminding him of the jowly, drooling dog, so I too was called Daisy. In the eyes of my proud father, I was the most beautiful baby in the whole wide world. My mother on the other hand saw me as a doll to be played with, dressed up, and shown off at every occasion. She left me in the care of my father in Trieste, Italy, where I was born, while she went back to dancing, thus contributing to the family income.

For me, life was uncomplicated, and I smiled, basking in my parents' love, and screamed whenever other people came near me. My parents, however, found life in Trieste very hard, as Hitler's shadow began to extend to all corners of Europe.

After much discussion and letter writing, my parents took me to Yugoslavia, where my father had an ex-mistress who was willing to help him and his family. She found accommodation for us, and my parents tried to find some kind of work. This proved to be in vain, so, sadly, we went on our travels again.

This time my father tried Czechoslovakia, for after all he was a Czech. At the frontier, guards tried to refuse us entry, but my father said that he was a relative of President Edvard Benesh, who would be most upset to have any of his family refused entry. After much discussion, we were permitted to enter Czechoslovakia and travelled to Prague, where my uncle Wilhelm joined us. My parents thought the time had come to marry, and thus, apart from making me legitimate, it made life easier for my mother, who automatically became a Czech citizen too.

Once again, life was good, and the fates smiled upon my parents, who found a lovely flat and both got jobs with the theatre. My father produced various musicals at the Deutsche Theatre—the German Theatre. He was offered a number of film productions, as well as jobs broadcasting on the German-language radio.

My mother had been given various parts in films, danced in musicals at the theatre, and generally worked on the stage at whatever part was offered to her. She was very beautiful and popular.

When my parents first moved to Prague, I was about a year old and quite a doll. My mother dressed me in the latest fashions and showed me off wherever she went. My father and Uncle Wilhelm looked after me with the help of a Czech nanny.

Once, when I was about two years old, my mother was playing with me on the floor of the flat, and when the front door bell rang she went to answer the door. I started screaming and would not stop even when my mother returned. She thought I was just naughty and screaming for attention. However, it transpired that somehow or other I had managed to break my arm and had to be rushed to hospital. For the next six weeks, I proudly wore a plaster cast on my right arm. I think that the fact of having a cast on my right arm made me use my left hand more, and since then I often appear confused as to which is my right and left hand. I now use either hand with equal ease. Later, Hitler forbade left-handedness in children, and we were all made to use our right hands. I had to be careful to use only my right hand for tasks like sewing, cutting, or writing and for all things at school.

When I was about three years old, my parents moved to a larger and more luxurious flat. I still have some vague recollections of it. It was on the third floor of a big apartment block, with large, lofty rooms. The staircase up to the flat was big with black wrought-iron banisters.

It was there that I first began to 'fly' in my dreams. I would spread my little arms and take a jump from the top step, waving the arms as if they were wings, and landing at the bottom of the first flight of stairs. I remember these dreams as clearly as if they had taken place today. I loved 'flying'.

When Saint Nicholas, the patron saint of all children came on the fifth of December, it was a custom to leave presents for good children and coal for naughty ones. I remember looking for my present between the two window panes—all flats had this double glazing with double windows, one set opening out and the other one opening inward.

I searched all the window places in the sitting room and all around the flat, but all I found was a lump of coal. I shed bitter tears. I had not been that naughty!

It was usual for the caretaker of the apartments to dress up as St Nicholas, wearing a bishop's garments and a bishop's mitre, and then go round knocking on all the flat doors, where children lived, accompanied by a person dressed up as the devil, who rattled his chains. When they knocked at our door, I was still crying and promised to be good. I was then told to check yet again all the windowsills and soon found a little cardboard dog filled with sweeties. Oh, how happy I was. I could not stop laughing and smiling.

Another memory that I have of living in that flat was being in the sitting room with my father, who was lighting the iron stove, which heated the living room. The stove was situated exactly opposite the French window leading onto the balcony. Suddenly my father cried out in pain and was unable to move. My mother came running and said he had *Hexenschuss*, which translated from the German means 'a shot from a witch' (lumbago or a slipped disc in English). I jumped up and ran to the window wanting to catch the bad witch who dared hurt my daddy, but there was no ne to be seen. I hugged my daddy and said I would take care of him. How I loved my daddy!

My mother used to take me out to the park so that I could play with the other children, but I was only used to being with adults and was therefore a most unsociable child when with my peers. Before long, I managed to drive all other children screaming back to their mothers or nannies. I then had the sandpit to myself and played happily by myself. Always interested in cooking, I loved to collect worms, which I then chopped up to make macaroni. The other children looked on but had no wish to join my macabre play and never played with me. What a little horror I must have been.

One day, when I was four years old, I was playing in the sitting room, when I suddenly heard my father's voice on the radio and ran up to it shouting 'Here I am daddy. Can you hear me? I can hear you!'

My father had been reading stories on a children's hour and then talked to the children. I could not fathom how he could not hear me when I could hear him loud and clear.

To get me to be more social and play with other children, my parents sent me to a Kindergarten. I remember enjoying going, there but my memories are hazy. One occasion, I do remember very clearly, must have touched me greatly. One of the children in the nursery had swallowed a penny whistle and choked to death and we all had to attend the funeral. I took with me a bunch of large bunch of daisies, well actually they were Margaritas—ox-eye daisies—and one by one we had to walk up to the plank that was put over the grave and then throw the flowers onto the coffin. This memory is still very clear in my mind, and I can see it all as if it were yesterday. To this day, I am nervous when children put small items into their mouth, in case they, too, choke and die.

Not only was I always dressed in the latest fashion, but also so were my dolls. We had the same patent black shoes, little suits, bows in our hair, and looked as if we had just stepped out of the shop window. I was never allowed to be dirty or scruffy—just had to be a little lady. Whenever I met an adult or was introduced to adults, I had to perform a deep curtsy and smile brightly.

At this time, I continued my nightly 'flying' in my dreams. As before, I would stand on the landing on the top stair and take a big jump, thus gliding down the first flight of stairs. As I got more proficient, I could actually fly down more and more flights of stairs, until I could manage all three floors and arrived at the bottom safe and sound. That was the beginning to my dream flights, which became more complicated as I grew older. They still continue to this very day.

Now that I was 'a big girl' and had at times been able to take small parts in certain musicals and films, it was time to make my stage debut. It was in a musical called the *Pfingst Orgel* (The Whitsun Organ). All I remember now was my beautiful costume, my singing and dancing, and that I seemed very popular. I had many curtain calls when I had to curtsey and received flowers and had sweets thrown at me on stage. I loved every moment of it. I, too, wanted to be a star like my wonderful and popular mother.

Exciting days and nights, bright lights, films, rides at the fun fair, and being every ones darling sadly soon came to an end as life's merry-go-round suddenly stopped when Hitler annexed Czechoslovakia and all Jews were being rounded up. We all had to wear the yellow Star of David on our sleeves and give up all but the most menial tasks of work. My parents left Prague and visited Brno where we had some distant relatives, who I had never seen before. When we arrived at their house, they immediately fell in love with me, as they could have no children on their own.

We stayed for a week, and then it was time to leave yet again. My relatives said they would miss me as I was such a lovely, bright, little girl. My mother then offered to leave me with them, although I did not know them at all, which must have been very traumatic for me. I have no recollection of that time at all, but I think I must have thought that I had been naughty to be given away so easily. Both my parents then left, and I had no idea whether I would ever see them again. Oh, why could my mother not love me? I always tried so hard to please her. I stayed some eight weeks there, and then, my mother suddenly returned and decided to take me to Germany to her mother, my grandmother. I was five years old but had never seen any of my relatives in Germany. Once again, it was a traumatic change in my short life.

There was no sign of my father, and he was never mentioned again, even when I cried for him. I was not allowed to talk about him or ask any questions. I was very bewildered not knowing why my beloved father, who loved me so much, had suddenly deserted me.

Being young, I adjusted to each change and soon found the train journey into Germany very exciting. We travelled by train from Prague to Pegnitz in Bavaria, where my grandmother lived.

Pegnitz was a large village or very small country town surrounded by woods, hills and countryside but it was also an important railway junction. My Aunt Agnes met our train and the two sisters greeted each other very warmly, kissing and hugging each other. I hid behind my mother's back, watching everything. As I looked on, I noticed a little face peering out from behind my aunt's back. Suddenly, my mother remembered my presence and proudly pulled me forward. I was dressed in the latest Prague fashion and was presented to my aunt, who in turn brought forward my cousin, dressed in Bavarian garb of leather trousers and jacket and a hat with a feather in it, and introduced him to my mother. The two sisters had not seen each other for quite a few years, and neither knew of the existence of children. My cousin and I just stared at each other—quite speechless. Oh, our mothers had so much to tell each other and with much hugging, laughing, crying, and constant talking walked off together hand in hand, forgetting us. So my cousin and I followed. It transpired that my cousin, a boy called Schorsch—the Bavarian for George—was one year younger than I and had his birthday five days before mine. From the first moment that we looked at each other, we loved each other—a love that would go on forever. I guess we recognised a need for each other as someone we could relate to and love.

We walked through the village, under the railway arches, and up the High Street until we came to my other aunt's home. That day was a grand reunion for the three sisters and my grandmother. There was so much to tell of the past. My aunts had married and divorced. My grandmother too had married, more as a convenience than a love match. My Aunt Emmi had prepared supper, and all the family—except the 'grandfather' who remained an outsider to the family—sat together and talked deep into the night. My cousin and I were left to our own devices, almost forgotten by our mothers and everyone else. Marvelling at all this excitement, love, hugging, laughter, and storytelling, we sat holding hands and fell asleep on the sofa.

Sometime during that evening, it was decided that I would go and live with my Aunt Emmi, who at that time lived alone, as she was childless and her husband was away fighting somewhere on the Russian Front. My aunt only had two rooms. One she used as a bedroom and the other one was the kitchen, living room, and bathroom (when we boiled water for the weekly bath and filled the tin tub for bathing). I was allocated a tiny broom cupboard with no window as my bedroom but often crept into bed with my aunt.

All the rooms were heated by freestanding, iron stoves that burned wood. We only lit the one in the living room, which was used for cooking as well as heating. In winter, my aunt would heat up bricks to put into our beds in order to warm them, as we had no hot-water bottles. The bedding was lovely and cosy with great big feather beds that one could really cuddle into and make a warm nest with no draughts.

Sometimes, when my aunt was cooking rice or pasta, she would wrap up the saucepan, once it had boiled, in a blanket and put it into the feather bed to continue cooking—thus saving on fuel. The toilet was shared by other families in the house and was situated on a balcony along a shared passage way. It was just a bench seat with a hole and the faeces would drop straight down onto a dung heap. There was no light, and it was scary to use the toilet at night. I was terrified to use it as I thought some evil creature might pull me down into the gloomy, smelly depth. At night, I refused to go there at all and preferred to use a chamber pot. How different things were at my aunt's from our lovely modern apartment in Prague.

The house was one of the old ones in the village and shared with other families. Life was very primitive but full of fun.

My Aunt Agnes lived with her son, Schorsch, only a few doors away, while my grandmother shared a very small flat with her husband a little further off.

I was made very welcome and was hugged by everyone when I was told that I would from that moment on stay in Pegnitz with my aunts and grandmother while my mother had to return to Prague. I did not mind, because suddenly, I had a cousin and two loving aunts, so that I felt quite at home there. I felt I was wanted.

However I was warned never again to mention my father, as he was Jewish and that was bad. I would be killed at once if anyone got to know that I had a Jewish relative of any sort. I was threatened never to talk about my past, or very bad things would happen to me and I would be shot. I also had to change my name from Daisy, which was an English name, to Margarita (Margaret). So with a new identity and a fresh start in life, I settled into being a real Bavarian dirndl, wearing real Bavarian dresses and no longer had to be the prim, little, fashionable miss.

After the short but passionate reunion with her family, my mother bid me goodbye and warned me to remember what I had been told and never to speak of my past life in Prague with her and my father. She left to go back to Prague, and there, unknown to me, she and my father decided to divorce so that we would not all be tainted with the same Jewish brush and I could be safe in Germany. As I said, I knew nothing of all this and never saw my father again and no one ever mentioned his name. That part of my life was over, and all was silence.

Chapter 2

Life in Bavaria was wonderful and free—a perfect dream for young children.

Oh, those beautiful, endless, hot, sunny summer days that followed. My childhood started in earnest, and I could not have been happier. My cousin and I were inseparable and spent all and every day and often most of the night in each other's company. My aunts were caring and loving but never showed any physical affection or feelings. My grandmother had never had time to cuddle her children and make a fuss of them, so in turn my mother and my aunts knew no better, not having had a good role model.

However, my cousin and I were very happy knowing that we were loved and basked in that warm, loving glow that this knowledge gave us.

War had broken out, and most men in Germany had been called up, so that work previously done by menfolk now had to be taken over by the women.

My great-aunt Haase, who owned several cinemas in various places, also owned the only cinema in Pegnitz. As there were no men about to look after the cinema, my aunts had to attend courses in film projection and management of the machinery, so that they could take over the screening of the films. This they did most proficiently, while my grandmother sat in the little office and worked as a cashier. Films were shown every evening, except Sundays, so my family was occupied, and my cousin and I were free to amuse ourselves. Every morning, my aunts and both my cousin and I had to go and clean, sweep, and tidy up the cinema, the toilets, and the little ticket office, making ready for the next performance. My grandmother collected all lost handkerchiefs dropped during the weepy films, so that she could take them home, boil, wash, and iron them and then give them to people as presents. We all had our tasks to perform. My cousin and I had to pick up all the rubbish and then sweep the floors, after which we were free once more to pursue our childhood games.

Because my aunts were working, my grandmother cooked all meals, and we all met in her place to eat. Only when sleeping were we separated. My grandmother was an excellent cook, so all meals were a real treat.

Once free of our tasks of cleaning, shopping, or running errands, my cousin and I were able to roam the countryside, go and play in the woods, and generally play around. Every evening, while the aunts were busy at the cinema, Schorsch and I would creep up to the cinema, enter via the toilet windows, which we had always left open in readiness, and when the theatre was in darkness, we would creep in, almost on our bellies, and watch every film—never mind the ratings. We made sure we were never caught by the police or anyone else. During the interval, we would disappear back into the toilet or hide behind the curtain where there was a little door leading to a flat above the cinema. Thus, we saw every film being shown several times, so that the next day we could re-enact the story on our little private stage. We changed parts regularly and never worried about gender. Therefore, I could be the hero or heroine, the dancer, the acrobat, Shirley Temple or even Zorro or other swashbuckling film stars. Nothing was impossible for us. We were in our element. Our aunts knew what we were up to, but as long as we caused no trouble, they pretended not to know what we were doing.

On Sunday afternoons, children's films were shown and we could legally attend, sitting like lords in the best seats. The films were mainly beautiful fairy stories, and we were truly enthralled. Fantasy and magic were right up our street, and we could re-enact everything there the next day, using scarves, old curtains, and hats as our costumes. Sometime later, my grandmother moved into the cinema flat, as it was more convenient to keep an eye on the place and do the maintenance. One of her sisters, who was sick, came to stay to be nursed by my grandmother. She stayed in bed in a little spare bedroom and we sometimes had to bring her food. Having been told that she had cancer (translated into "crab" in German), we were both curious and frightened, as we imagined little crabs crawling all around her bed and blankets. We avoided any contact with her.

Now that my grandmother lived in the cinema flat, it made life even easier for Schorsch and I to go scrumping, as it gave us access to the garden, filled with summer fruits, and there was plenty of space to play. We made the garden our own, only to be chased out by the 'grandfather' who would throw shoes and wood at us from time to time and go on his way, shouting and complaining all the time. We just laughed and disappeared for the time being, ready to re-emerge at a later time when the coast was clear. Apart from these occasional set-tos, we never met the 'grandfather' or had anything to do with him. All in-laws were kept as outlaws in our family, and our grandmother would have nothing to do with them. So our uncle, Aunt Emmi's husband, when he did eventually come back from the war was always referred to by his surname, Wohleben, and was kept at a distance.

Some evenings, my aunts decided to lock us in so we would go to bed early, but as my Aunt Agnes lived in a ground floor flat so we would climb out of the windows and continue our play and adventure activities. Other evenings, we would invent games and competitions to amuse ourselves. On one of these occasions we had a competition as to who could aim farthest when peeing. We stood on the windowsill, leaned backwards, and tried to see who the winner was. I doubled backwards as far as I could, so that I had better aim, and we both managed a draw—how, I do not know. Perhaps my cousin took pity on a girl who had no willy to use as a hosepipe.

We were never short of new ideas.

During the summer months, my aunts tried to earn extra money by managing the outdoor swimming pool. Their task was to open up each morning, keep the place clean, sell refreshments, and generally work until evening, when it was time to go and open up the cinema. Schorsch and I would go with the aunts to help with cleaning and shopping. We loved to go shopping, as we always received sweets or biscuits from the shopkeepers, and when going to the butcher, we would receive the off cuts of delicious sausage and salami.

Sometimes, we were sent to the nearby brewery to fetch crates of bottled beer and take them back to the swimming pool in a wheelbarrow. Having completed our tasks, we were then free to swim and splash about in the water. In fact, both Schorsch and I taught ourselves to swim and how to dive off the high diving board. Fearless, we became very proficient at swimming. My aunts would bring food for lunch to the swimming pool, or sometimes my cousin and I had to go and collect a hot dinner that my grandmother had cooked. Thus, we always had something scrumptious to eat. My aunts made ice cream and refreshments that they sold, so extra treats would sometimes come our way. The summers seemed endless and hot and full of fun and adventure. War and the persecution of Jews were far away, and we were all quite unaware of what was happening elsewhere in Germany.

Chapter 3

When I was six-years-old, I had to start school and was duly enrolled in the village school. The first day of school life is a very important one in Germany and celebrated as such. On their first school day, each child is presented with a huge two or even three—foot paper cornet stuffed full of goodies. There were coloured pencils, pencils, rulers, fruit, toys, and sweets. We were also given a new slate and graphite pencil, which we would use for all our writing and arithmetic. On the first day, we were all taken to school and a special celebration was held to welcome us to the academic life. Songs were sung and dances performed. We met our teachers and after two hours were sent home again, to start school in earnest the following day. This special occasion was of course commemorated by the taking lots of photographs.

I was quite a popular girl, perhaps due to the fact that the children knew I was a 'townie' from Prague and spoke 'posh'. It did not take long for me to lose my Prague accent and to learn the Bavarian dialect, and as I out grew my town clothes, I could dress in Bavarian dirndls—the same as everyone else. I hated to be different from the others and therefore adapted very quickly and fitted in to my new surroundings. I had learnt to be like a chameleon.

My cousin and I were always referred to as the cinema children (ours being the only cinema for miles, or should I say kilometres around), which gave us added respect. School was only every morning, from seven to twelve, so that we had plenty of time to enjoy our own special pastimes. My cousin was a year younger than I and patiently awaited my return from school so that we could enjoy the cinema, swimming, and all our open-air activities during those the endless, hot, summer days together.

Later that year, we would wake one morning, to a world suddenly changed as if by magic. Winter had arrived. The whole world had been transformed into fairyland. Everything glistened white, and all the trees were covered with 'icing sugar'. Snow had fallen, and the world appeared so silent and beautiful with the only sound to be heard was the crunch of snow underfoot. We could then go out on the toboggan or our skis and enjoy the winter sports on the slopes of the meadows or the woods. Oh, how happy we were. The story goes that Mrs Holle lived above the clouds and had servants whose job it was to shake out the big feather beds, and when they did their job well, it snowed on earth. We always sent a prayer up to Mrs Holle to send plenty of snow, although we then had more, new chores to do. We had to keep the pavements outside the flats and the cinema clear of snow. We made this into games and enjoyed shovelling the snow in order to clear the pavements and sprinkling sand to stop people slipping. Every householder was responsible for the area outside their door, and we were proud of the task allotted to us and made sure we had the best pavement area all round.

My mother came to visit whenever she had a holiday from work, and then the family's joy and my happiness would be complete.

Christmases were especially magic. On the fifth of December, Saint Nicholas's Day, we would hang up our stockings and wait for the evening to see whether St. Nicholas would come. It was custom for St Nicholas to appear, dressed in his red robe and bishop's mitre. He would question the children to see if they had been good and then reward them with presents, I remember very clearly St Nicholas coming to our living room where we were gathered for the celebration. My cousin and I were so frightened that we hid under the bed, and had to be asked to come out. It took a great deal of persuasion for us to reappear from under the bed. We then had to recite a poem and sing a song, but we were suspicious that St Nicholas was our Aunt Emmi, as he wore her ring. This caused much consternation before getting our presents. Once I was clutching my presents, I seemed to become bolder and cried and eventually laughed. Usually it would be a male member of the household or a friend who would dress up, but alas the men were at war, so the aunts had to do their best and a great time was had by all.

We both promised to be good children and do as our aunts bade us, so we received our St Nicholas presents.

With the coming of December, Advent time had arrived. We went to church, as we did every Sunday, lit the advent candles, and sang Christmas songs. Having attended Sunday school all the year round we knew all the Bible stories and enjoyed hearing the Christmas story all over again. No decorations were put up until Christmas Eve, but we prepared by shopping around the villages for black-market food for the Christmas dinner, did baking, and made secret presents for each other. What excitement reigned all about us.

On the evening of the twenty fourth of December, a tree would appear in the living room and would be lavishly decorated in our absence by the Christmas Angels. Presents appeared, brought by the Christ child, and were opened after we had come back from church, which we attended with all the family. It was wonderful walking back from church in the velvety darkness. Our way was lit by myriad of stars and the moon. All was still and silent, and the only sound to be heard was the crunch of the snow under foot. We arrived back home with bright red cheeks brought about by the cold wind and the mounting excitement. With eyes bright as round as saucers, we were awed by the lovely tree, decorated in silver and white with little biscuits and ornaments. The strips of foil, called lametta, twinkled in the light, and many white candles lit up the tree, which was covered in angel hair. Oh! How beautiful it all was!

First, we had the delicious meal that was laid out in festive style. Then, came the opening of presents by candlelight. We had such fun. We sang songs, recited poems, and grandmother would tell stories until late into the night.

The next morning, we had to attend church again, followed by more Christmas dinner—this time roast goose with all the trimmings. Life was good.

Oh, yes, we had the usual childhood illness of measles, coughs, and colds, and I even caught scarlet fever. These passed as quickly as they appeared.

One day, I had been naughty and was woken in the night to see a ghost in my bedroom. I screamed out loudly, and my aunt came rushing in. I had to admit to being naughty and promised to be good in future, before I could settle back to sleep. Later, I discovered that my aunt had hung up a bed sheet to dry in the room, and to me it had looked like a ghost—or, as I described it, the Virgin Mary—seen from the back.

Another time, I was really frightened when my grandmother, as usual, had told her numerous ghost stories, and I had to go to the toilet. As I said, my aunt lived in one of the oldest houses in the village, and we had to visit the balcony to perform the necessary. That night when I had to go to the toilet, I thought a ghost was pulling me down with his hands, so I would only go with my aunt in attendance.

With no television, it always fell to my grandmother to tell stories, which invariably ended with ghosts, dead people, and cemeteries, To this day, we all are afraid of cemeteries at night, dark alleys, and graves, where a hand could appear at any moment and pull us down into the grave. We still to this day look under the bed to see if anyone or anything would be there. We did not need horror films as Grandmother was a past master at telling chilling tales to the aunts, while we listened in horror but were nevertheless enthralled. When we had to walk past the nearby cemetery, we would make huge detours because we were afraid to meet one of the ghosts that we had heard so much about. During the day, things were different as ghosts only walked after midnight—the witching time of night when churchyards yawn and hell itself opens its doors.

During the day, the cemetery looked so beautiful with all the marble statues above each grave. There were many lovely angels with wings furled, keeping watch over the graves. There were trees and flowers everywhere, lending a festive air of remembrance. At night, however, the scene seemed to change to one of evil and foreboding. The angels seemed to take wing, and the trees stretched out their gnarled arms to catch the passer-by, while the dead bodies rose from their graves and every one of them joined in a macabre dance until the clock struck one when all returned to their graves. As I said, to this day I am still afraid to pass graveyards by night.

My aunts, on the other hand, would tell tales of fairies, witches, and goblins. Sometimes, they would sing Victorian songs that always ended in tragedy, and then we cried. When I hear some of these songs now, I cannot listen to them without crying.

Both my cousin's and my imagination were filled to the full and were so well developed with lively stories that were put to good use when acting out the different stories and films on our stage.

Chapter 4

The first we knew of any war was when we stood on our balcony and looked out one night to see the entire horizon filled with light and flashes as if a magnificent fireworks display was in progress. It was in fact the bombing of Nurnberg that we could see from a long way off. Aeroplanes fell burning from the sky, like some magical comets, and we stood in awe and watched the unfolding scene, not really comprehending what was happening.

Another time, while on one of our many adventurous explorations through the woods, my cousin and I came across a high wire fence, holding prisoners of war. I guess they were French, because we were told that they might be hungry and would be glad to have some snails to eat. So not wanting anyone to be hungry, we went on a snail hunt and gathered up as many snails as we could find and brought them to the wire fence, leaving them there for the prisoners to find. Later, we were told not to go near the prisoners again, and were frightened by stories of what might happen if we disobeyed. So we kept well clear of that wood and looked upon it as yet another adventure we had had.

My cousin and I were unaware of rationing or food shortages. My aunts, resourceful as ever, would go to nearby villages to barter with farmers or just buy special produce on the black market. We called it to go 'hamstering' after the little animal that would collect as much food as he could and then store it for a later time and for needy days.

These occasions were always great fun, as we would all go out very early in the morning and walk miles to outlying villages and collect all that the farmers would sell us. We also could enjoy a real farmer's breakfast, which was a real treat.

These forages into the country would always coincide with slaughter time, so food was plenty and a feast was set before us every time.

I hated when the farmer would ask my aunt to choose a chicken she wanted. The chosen chicken would then be caught and beheaded in front of our eyes. This I could never bear to watch. I did not think it funny to see a headless chicken trying to run away till it dropped. I soon learned when I had to look away.

Well stocked up for the next few months, we returned home triumphantly.

Then each autumn, there were the magical expeditions into the forest to gather wood for the winter, as all our rooms were heated by wood burners. My aunts hired a farm hand with horse and cart and we all drove out into the forest for the day. Wood was ordered previously, and we were told where to find our allocated pile of wood, cut into meter-long logs and stacked, awaiting our collection.

My cousin and I sat at the back of the cart like royalty and enjoyed the ride, as the horse clattered through the villages and then through forests. We sang as we went but became quiet when travelling through the dense, dark woods, with tall, silent trees. We were full of awe seeing all that beauty and thought any moment a goblin or fairy would appear. Some of the twisted, old trees seemed to take on a life of their own, and we thought they would come alive at any moment.

While my aunts loaded the cart, we played out our imaginary games, running and climbing around the forest but never out of sight of the aunts—just in case. You never knew who or what might materialize, especially when we found magic circles of mushrooms.

After a picnic with our favourite snacks we drove back home with my cousin and me balancing on top of the gathered wooden logs, which were neatly stacked on the cart. Outside our home, the wood had to be stored in neat piles, ready for cutting into foot-long pieces. For days after this event, my cousin and I had to take it in turn to chop the wood into smaller more manageable sizes, before storing them once more under the eaves of the house, in neat piles. All the wood had to be put in neat rows, and the side that was visible to the passer-by had to be tidy and all facing the same way. To this day, you can see the neat wall of chopped wood under the houses, keeping dry and ready to use in winter. We loved that job as it gave us a feeling of achievement and being grown up, and we were praised for all the effort we put into our tasks.

Often in the autumn, we would again be taken by the aunts into the woods, this time to gather mushrooms and blueberries, ready to store for the winter. That, too, was great fun, and we had to learn which mushrooms were eatable and which were poisonous. I can still smell the dank, damp earth of the cool forest, smell the fresh aroma of the tall pines, and taste the little, yellow, delicious mushrooms in my mouth. I loved mushroom gathering. We also collected buckets full of blueberries, eating as many as we could along the way. After completing our tasks, we enjoyed our Picnic, and then, tired and covered in blue juice from the blueberries that we had picked and eaten, we returned home. The mushrooms had then to be cleaned and laid out or hung up to be dried and kept until they were required. The fruit had be cooked and bottled as we had no refrigerators and freezers were not available to us.

Sometime during our idyllic life in the country, my uncle Wohleben, my Aunt Emmi's husband, returned from the Russian Front, invalided out because of severe frostbite. He had lost most of his toes. Although I continued living with my Aunt Emmi, in the tiny broom cupboard, I hardly saw my uncle, who was by now a morose, unfriendly man, whose only pleasure in life was to get drunk. Thus, every night he would disappear to some pub or other and drown his sorrows with his drinking pals. It was usually my task to go and find my uncle by searching through all the pubs in the area and then locate him. I always delivered the message that he was to come home and then went to report to my aunt where she could find him, as I was too small to take home an abusive, drunken man. I hated those dingy, smoky pubs, frequented mainly by old men, and the memory of the smoke and drink stayed with me forever. Now I just do not like pubs.

Life went on as before, my aunts working and my cousin and I enjoying life and freedom to the full. By then I had become a real country girl, speaking the broad Bavarian dialect and running around barefooted in Bavarian dresses. I was so happy that I wanted nothing to change. No, never, never, never.

Unexpectedly, my mother arrived one day, to tell me she was going to be married and that I would have to go back to Prague and live with her and my new father in a lovely new, large flat—in Prague named Holesovice. I did not know whether to be sad or happy, but when my mother reassured me that all my holidays would be spend in Bavaria with my aunts and cousin, I began to look forward to going back to Prague and be with my lovely mother again. Nothing was said of my own father, and I was not allowed to ask questions. I presumed him to be dead. I dared not ask any questions.

My grandmother went to Prague with my mother to get ready for the wedding, and I would be sent for in due course. I was very disappointed, as I had wanted to be a bridesmaid and wear a beautiful gown. Alas, it was not to be.

After my mother's wedding, my grandmother returned home and told us all the news and described the wedding in full. My mother looked really beautiful, like a real princess, and had been radiant with happiness. Her new husband was handsome and a real gentleman. They had newly furnished a grand flat and everything seemed set for a happy ever after.

Before long my mother sent a telegram requesting that I join her in Prague.

The day of my departure came all too soon. I had leave and live with my mother and stepfather. I wondered if stepfathers are as wicked as stepmothers are supposed to be. *We shall see*, I thought.

Sadly, I said goodbye to my school friends and promised to return the very next holiday. My cousin and I knew that this was not goodbye and promised to tell each other everything when we saw each other again.

The time for another chapter in my life had begun, little did I know that my magical and enchanted childhood in Bavaria had come to an abrupt end and soon I would have to face the harsh realities of life.

Chapter 5

My sad farewells over, I was put on the train by my aunts and was told that my mother would collect me on arrival at the station. They asked a train guard to keep an eye on me and see to it that I got out at the right place as it was a very long journey across the German and Czech borders, or should I say Sudetenland frontier, since Czechoslovakia had also been annexed by Hitler. I assured my aunts that I was a big girl of nearly eight years old and could look after myself. I hugged them and promised to come back as soon as I could and my mother would allow.

My mother and my new father were waiting for me as I stepped out of the train. I was welcomed by them both with big hugs and kisses. I took an immediate liking to my new father, who was a kind and good-looking man. We went home to our flat in a very nice neighbourhood. It was in a tall, modern building with a lift and was managed by a caretaker. We lived on the second floor. The flat was large, airy, and spacious, tastefully decorated and beautifully furnished with new furniture—a real luxury apartment. I was shown to my own room next to the kitchen. I suppose it would have been the maid's room if had we had one. There was a large bedroom, dining room, and sitting room, as well as a real bathroom and water closet and central heating! I thought this must all be a real film set, because in Bavaria we only had two rooms to live, bathe, cook, and sleep in. Now we also had two balconies. I loved the flat and felt immediately at home.

New clothes and toys awaited me. I clearly remember a tea set that I had, made of light aluminium. On each plate and cup was a different picture of the Dionne quintuplets—the five babies born to a Canadian family in 1934. I loved that tea set and played with it constantly. I also had new dolls with a special wardrobe that my stepfather had bought me. Books, coloured pencils, and other toys awaited me as well, so that I had plenty to occupy my time. I explored everything and was allowed to go down into the yard to play there with other children living in the block of flats.

My mother was horrified at the country bumpkin I had become and immediately set about to 'clean me up', by buying a new, up-to-date wardrobe for me and cut off my plats and then put my hair into rags to act as curlers, so I could have a Shirley Temple hairstyle. Cleaned and spruced up, with lovely summer dresses and dainty, black-leather shoes, I was more like the daughter she wanted.

For the winter, she had bought me an elegant woollen coat, trimmed with white rabbit fur, with a hat and collar to match, as well as a little white-fur muff to keep my hands warm. Cosy, felt, knee-high boots completed the outfit. I felt like a film star and did not complain when my mother had to brush out my hair after it had been in cloths or paper curlers. Beauty must suffer, she used to say as she brushed, scrubbed, and generally turned me into a little model girl. I also had to stop using my Bavarian accent, but had to talk 'proper' in High German, as befitted a young lady.

I loved being with my stepfather, who had a beautiful singing voice and who would often sing to me. By profession, he was a solicitor and worked at his father's office in the centre of Prague. He really wanted to be a musician and studied piano, singing, and music in general, in his spare time, but his father would have none of it and made him join the family business.

Sometime later, I was told of how it came about that my mother met him. She was travelling back from Bavaria by train and, being a very beautiful woman, was chatted up by a fellow traveller going the same way. His name was Fred, and he was greatly enamoured of my mother. They had lunch together on the train, and he told her that he was meeting his best friend at the station and would be greatly honoured if she would join them for dinner that night. The friend was Walter Decker who fell in love with my mother at first sight. The three of them went out frequently and became firm friends. Not long after, my mother announced her engagement to this charming man, Walter, who then became my stepfather.

I met the new in-laws when my mother took me to their home. There was the old lady, Mrs Decker, and her husband as well as the two daughters (married and by then divorced) called Magda and Hertha, who had a son of my age called Horst. I did not take to my new grandparents, and I think that the feeling was mutual. Magda and I became good friends but Hertha, a very masculine woman, did not warm to me.

While my parents had to work, I was taken to the in-laws to be looked after and play with Horst. Often, I would be told off for leading him astray and had to take all the blame for anything naughty that he did. I was the stepdaughter of their son and thus an outsider, however hard I tried to please them and become one of the family. Horst was always showered with presents and chocolates, and I remember wanting desperately to share some of the goodies but had to invent games where he could reward me with the chocolates and thus I got my fair share. I got on quite well with him, but it was more of having no choice to do otherwise.

The in-laws had a Czech maid, who befriended me and became my ally, and I made myself useful in the household by helping her with some chores, hoping to be praised by my step grandmother. Alack, no. She never showed any interest in me, and I was just a duty she had to perform to keep her son happy. I became reserved and kept out of the way, not wanting to offend anyone.

In the larger world Hitler was enlisting all the young men in the Sudetenland to send them into war. Fred and my stepfather were duly drafted and sent to fight for the Fatherland on the Western Front. Once more my mother was left on her own to manage as best she could.

I was enrolled at a very good German school, which had a grammar school attached to it, and I enjoyed going there very much. It was some way off from our home, so every day I had to take a tram to get there. School on the Continent was only every morning, thus I had yet again to go to the in-laws place in the afternoon, until my mother could collect me to take me home, where I could once again play with the other children in the yard. I quickly learnt the Czech language and became a fluent speaker. No one could tell I was German. As always, like a chameleon, I changed my 'colour' and fitted in with the others and my immediate surroundings.

The school curriculum was wide and varied, and I particularly enjoyed music, art, and needlework. I learned to knit and crochet, which allowed me to make nice presents for my mother at Christmas. We also went on several school outings, visiting famous palaces and other interesting historic places.

We also played many games at school, and I loved joining in everything. I did well at school and was a keen pupil. I was popular with my peers and joined their games at break time. There was no school uniform, and we could all wear whatever we pleased. The atmosphere in the school was one of enjoyment and everyone was kind and friendly. That however did not mean that discipline was lax. On the contrary, we had to behave and were punished when naughty. I received my fair amount of punishment, like everyone else. If too chatty in class, the teacher stuck some adhesive strip over my mouth, or at other times I would receive the cane. I was called out in front of the class and had to hold out my hand, palm upwards. The cane whistled as it descended through the air and then landed on my hand with a loud clap. Oh, how my hand stung and tears came into my eyes, but I never made a sound, as that was not accepted by my peers. We all accepted these punishments and thought them well deserved, and no one ever bore a grudge. School life continued in a happy and carefree way, and we all loved going there every day.

Coming from a Catholic family, it was soon time for me to learn my catechism and then take my first communion. Every Sunday, while my mother had a lie in, I travelled by tram to the old part of Prague where the church was. There I learnt my religious lessons and helped with the flower decorations and tried to join in singing in the choir. At last, the day of my communion approached. This is an exciting day for a little Catholic girl, and I was dressed in a white dress and veil, just like a little bride, and received a large, decorated candle. When I was thus attired, my mother came with me to church to witness this auspicious occasion.

The church was a beautiful, old church near the St Charles Bridge on the bank of the river Moldau. From there, you got a magnificent view of the Hradcany—the old castle. This old part of Prague dated back to the Middle Ages with its narrow cobbled streets and houses where alchemists tried to make gold. I was truly honoured to be able to take my first communion in that lovely part of town and in such a historic church. In fact, I loved every bit of Prague, with all its baroque and renaissance churches, palaces, imposing theatres, its wide avenues, the majestic river, and the many parks. I was so proud to be living in that wonderful city, often referred to as the jewel box of Europe.

After my first communion and the indoctrination into the Catholic Church, I became very religious, and while my mother would sleep, I would travel to the church in order to attend morning service and became an altar girl, helping decorating the altar, was then able to join the church choir and generally help preparing for each Sunday service. Even when very cold in winter, with snow blizzards blowing, I would keep on my pyjamas, put on my garments over the top, and make my way to church. I never missed a service, and I vowed to become a nun. I guess I fancied the nun's costume and liked to spend my time in beautiful churches, all full of lavish, gold decorations, fantastic stained glass windows, and paintings by old masters, with fragrant flowers everywhere and echoing with great music. What a beautiful life that would be. I would also be able to help all the poor people and the homeless children and give my life to God.

However, that wish would have to wait for a while.

Being eight-years-old, I was obliged to join the Hitler Youth and was duly kitted out in my new uniform. How proud I was wearing my uniform. I had never had one before as children in Continental schools did not wear any uniform. I joined a local pack, and I loved going to the weekly meetings where we sang songs, were told stories, and made various things in our handicraft sessions that we later took to the children's hospital as presents and where we sang and entertained the sick children.

My mother was not at all happy about my having had to join the Hitler Youth and often forbade me to go. I made the maid write me an excuse on notepaper and returned to the Hitler Youth as often as I could, when my mother was not about. I really loved the sessions and was lucky that our pack leader did not indoctrinate us with Hitler's ideas and politics. I suppose that my pack was rather like joining the Girl Guides or Brownies in England,

Of course, I had to go to confession in church, and offer special prayers for disobedience and deceit. After so many Hail Marys, I was forgiven—till next time.

Now that my mother was all on her own again, I felt it my duty to look after her in every way I could. I ran errands, went shopping, helped in the house, and became her 'little sister'. Speaking Czech fluently helped me a great deal when going to the different shops. She discussed all her worries and problems with me, and although I could not solve any of them, I suppose that I was a useful tool by just being there listening, so that she could get everything off her chest. I felt responsible for her as she was a woman on her own.

When I was naughty, however, my mother remembered that I was a little girl, and I received a thrashing with her wooden spoon. One day, knowing I was in for a beating, I ran out of the flat, knowing she would not run after me and beat me in public. Crouching in the hall, I waited for her temper to recede, but alas, knew that I would still receive my punishment and in the end crawled back home and took what was coming. When I went to bed that night, my mother tried to make it up to me by giving me a special treat of bread and margarine with mustard on it, or at other times, sugar sprinkled on it. Yum, yum, these were great treats.

I loved my little room but only went to sleep if my mother left the door open, so that light would shine in, and I would not be in darkness. I also liked to hear the radio and would go to sleep while listening to it.

I tried to please my mother in every way I could and therefore did not make too much fuss when she dressed me in beautiful clothes and combed my Shirley Temple ringlets. I was always the young lady in the city instead of the tomboy that I preferred to be, running free in the open air with my cousin. Well, I could leave my tomboy days for the holidays that I would spend in Germany.

My mother had become a heavy smoker, and as everything was rationed, she could never get enough cigarettes to last her. I had heard that one could buy cigarettes on the black market at the Prague Railway stations, so in order to please and surprise her I set off travelling to the centre of town, where the main station was situated. It was evening and dark, so that not so many people were about, but nevertheless the station was very busy. I was extremely nervous and frightened by all the strange-looking people and the eerie atmosphere; however, I plucked up my courage and wandered around the vast station, surreptitiously asking where or from whom I could buy some black-market cigarettes. I was sent from one weird-looking person to another. Now, I think of it as a scene straight from one of Charles Dickens's novels.

In the dark, mist, and smoke of the station, I eventually found a man who would sell me what I was after. He acted very furtively and took me to a dark corner to question me. I was terrified, but thinking of how pleased my mother would be, I followed him and told him my story. He smiled, pattered me on the head, and I then exchanged money for the sought after little parcel.

Relieved and victorious, I returned home, to find a worried mother who had wondered where I could have got to. She was not sure whether to be angry or pleased, but in the end hugged me and said how clever I was. She warned me never to go there again, as it was dangerous for a small girl to be out in the dark. However the cigarettes did not last forever, and since I had made a good contact, my mother let me go foraging for more tobacco on other numerous occasions. I was overjoyed to be able to do this for her, as I wanted her to be happy and love me. So I forgot my fears and continued my black-market activity and visited the dark corners of the smoky train station, where I became known as the little cigarette girl. If one man had nothing to sell, I was sent to another one, and thus never came back home empty handed. As these excursions always had to take place in the dark, I soon learned to look after myself and avoid trouble when I saw it.

My mother and I were such good friends that it was difficult for me to realize that she was my mother as it was she who always needed my help, instead of me needing mothering and reassurance.

One day, we heard that my stepfather had been taken prisoner of war by the English and was now on the Island of Alderney, where he gave concert recitals and was even heard on the BBC when they broadcast from there. He was in his element, as he loved music so much and was a gifted tenor singer, as well as a promising pianist.

Chapter 6

Later that year, a surprise visitor arrived at our flat. Uncle Fred was on special leave and came to see how my mother was getting on. He stayed a few days with us, and when hearing him make certain advances to my mother, I had the strong feeling that this should not be so. Although I was very naive and knew nothing about sex cried out, pretending to be disturbed in my sleep, so that my mother had to attend to me and could not continue her sexual flirtations with Fred. Disheartened and disappointed because I spoilt his fun, he left shortly afterwards.

Poor Mum—I now know better and should have let her have a little bit of fun, as she so needed the adulation of men as well as their company.

My teeth needed a check-up, so my mother took me to a dentist specializing in children's dentistry. However, I was stubborn and did not want to go to the dentist. I was in fact terrified. Once pushed into the room and asked to sit in the dentist's chair, I just refused to open my mouth. No amount of cajoling would persuade me, and when the dentist used force, I just bit him and consequently was thrown out and my mother was told never to darken his door again, as I was a monster.

War was a long way off for us, and I knew nothing about such things. We did have rationing and we all had to be fitted with gas masks, but I just took all that in my stride and thought it the norm. Wearing a gas mask seemed like a game—like being some creature from another world—and that made us laugh. Life was good, and we had a lot of fun.

At last, the school holidays came and my mother, as promised, put me on the train to Bavaria, where my cousin and aunts collected me from the station. I sat by the train window and looked out at the passing countryside. The wheels of the train kept repeating 'just a few more kilometres, just a few more kilometres and then you'll be there'. At last, the countryside outside became familiar, and I recognised various landmarks. Before long, the train pulled into the Pegnitz station, and I saw my cousin waving madly and my aunt was there with outstretched arms, ready to welcome me. I was so happy to be back in Bavaria once again.

Then followed more glorious summer and later winter days, when Schorsch and I continued our adventures as if I had never gone away. My aunts were always pleased to see me as was our grandmother, although she rarely showed any affection. As soon as I arrived, I stripped off my city clothes and once more became the free-spirited Bavarian girl, dropping the posh German speech and speaking only in broad Bavarian dialect. The holiday ended far too quickly, but my cousin and I knew that before long I would return again and again.

On my return home to Prague, I was due for a surprise: my mother was expecting a baby and we were all delighted. In due course, a baby girl, named Sylvia Ingrid, was born, and she was the sweetest little thing I had ever seen. Her head was covered in tight, dark-brown curls, and she was so cuddly and sweet. I loved to help my mother look after her and just adored my little sister. My stepfather was delighted with the news and only wished he could see his little daughter. The Christening was a serious but joyous occasion, with all the in-laws and even my grandmother from Bavaria attending.

I helped with the bathing of the baby and took her for walks in the park. How I loved the tiny thing.

Some days, my mother would take us both to the park, and she often recounted the story of how a group of soldiers out on a march were suddenly halted in front of her and were asked to pass water. The sergeant did this on purpose to shock and embarrass my mother, seeing all these men pee, but she never turned a hair and only laughed. It made a good story for years to come.

Another time, while walking with my mother, a little dog on a lead just jumped up and bit my thigh without any reason at all. I still have the scar and have been frightened of dogs ever since, making big detours so as not to meet any dog at all—big or small.

I grew tall, strong, and healthy and knew how to adapt to being Bavarian or the smart city girl in Prague.

Now that my mother could no longer work, having a baby to look after, she would sometimes, during my school holidays, come to Bavaria with me. On one of these occasions, she offered to take my country bumpkin of a cousin back to Prague with us, so that he too could benefit from a good school and learn some civilised manners in the town. My aunt agreed, and I was delighted for Schorsch to be offered such a good opportunity of excellent schooling and be able to experience life in beautiful Prague with us.

He must have found everything very strange: no cinema, no open-air pool, and no endless freedom. However, he soon settled into town life, and we made up new and different adventures, visiting various places of interest, exploring parks, and inventing games to play in our yard. Of course, we had our quarrels and disagreements. I remember one day arguing with my cousin and my mother took his part, so I sulked and would not go to share my bed with him. All night I sat in the kitchen, on the stone floor with my back against the radiator. Of course, we in Prague had central heating and did not have to light wood burners. Unfortunately, the heating went off in the early hours and I got colder and colder until I had to give in and creep into bed with Schorsch. By the next day, all was forgotten and we were best of friends again. Again life seemed promising and was good.

Suddenly, one day the war caught up with us as a bomb fell in Prague. This was an unheard of occurrence. Everyone rushed to the place where it was dropped to see what had happened, as this was something new to the inhabitants of Prague. My cousin and I were on our way back from school when we heard the news. Of course, we too had to go and see the disaster area and made our way there by bus. It was not very exciting as one could only see rubble where a house had been. No gore or blood. Disappointed, we went back home to be told off by a worried mother, who had heard about the bomb and did not know where we were.

During a visit of an important dignitary who was making a State visit to Prague, I got caught up in the throng and went to see if I could get a view of the famous man. I stood on tiptoes to see him, when a pervert tried to grab my bottom. Outraged, I ran for the tram and went back home to tell my mother. She laughed and told me not to worry but I was right to get back home quickly.

My cousin and I missed the cinema, so my mother would allow us to visit a local playhouse to see certain films. Very different to the times we climbed in through the toilet window and saw all films. However, it was good to be in make-believe land once more.

The film that made the biggest impression on me was about a children's specialist called 'Doktor Engel' (Doctor Angel). He was tall, handsome, empathic, and loved by everyone—a sort of Dc Kildare but only working in a children's hospital. From that day on, being a nun flew out of the window, and I vowed I wanted to become a paediatrician and my interest in medicine was kindled. We went to see that film many times and of course re-enacted it at home until I knew all the medical jargon by heart.

Christmas came, and Aunt Agnes came to Prague to celebrate with us, seeing that her son was living with us. Time passed very quickly, and she had to return once more, promising to come back in the summer and collect both of us to return with her to Bavaria.

Once again, fate had a different future for us in mind.

CHAPTER 7

WE WOKE UP ONE SUNNY morning, and as usual, I was sent shopping. First, carrying my litre enamelled can to fetch the milk from the dairy shop where I would buy a litre of fresh milk. There were no milk carts or milk deliverymen.

Then I had to go to the baker and then the local butcher to complete my task. I always spoke Czech when shopping and enjoyed the encounter with all the shopkeepers, who were very friendly and jovial. Visiting the butcher was always a pleasurable task, as he was very welcoming, and I always received the off cuts of the sausages to eat on my way home. No wonder that to this day I still love my German sausages and salamis.

As I entered the shop that morning, I heard angry, raised voices. The usually so friendly butcher was brandishing his long, sharp knives and shouting that he would kill every German he could find. Everyone else joined in the angry outcries against the Germans.

No one noticed me, and in any case had always looked upon me as a little Czech girl, hearing me only speak in Czech when shopping. I paled visibly under the onslaught of menacing words and proposed actions and hastily sidled out of the shop unnoticed and ran home to my mother as fast as I could to breathlessly relate what had happened. She immediately put on the radio in order to hear the news. There too was much commotion and shouting on the air and angry voices were raised in a frenzy. Then followed sharp gunshots, and the announcement came that the German Radio station was now under Czech control. It was announced that the war was at an end and the Germans had lost, but they tried to make a last stand here in Prague. There was bombing in the old town, which could be heard both on the air and as echoes from across the city. We were told that the French, American, and Russian tanks were joining forces and were advancing toward the city of Prague in order to seize the power. There was chaos everywhere, and fear could be smelled in the air.

My mother immediately began to pack necessary items into a suitcase, collected some food, and bade us to keep clear of windows and stay out of sight. We, too, packed our most important belongings, as the caretaker of the block of flats had come to warn us that an uprising was in progress and we had better go below into the cellars so as to be safe. Already we could hear gunshots in our neighbourhood, and the tall building shook as bombs fell. There was smoke everywhere. The Allies were converging in Prague city centre. We rushed below into the cellars where others had already gathered, huddling together in fear. The cellar was cold and dark with just a small light so as not to arouse any attention to the fact that we were hiding there.

We had to stay in the cellar for many days and huddled in blankets and tried to get some sleep. The shooting and bombing seemed to continue for what seemed like most of the week. Daily, my mother sent me up to the flat to warm milk for my baby sister and get some food for us. My cousin accompanied me in order to give me courage. We crept upstairs on all fours, like soldiers in the trenches, and went into our flat. Hearing shots, we crept up to the windows to see what was going on. Hearing more gunshots, we saw people firing and therefore hastily withdrew and completed the task of getting the food.

We returned to the cellars to hear more angry talk and shouting. People proposed building barricades against the oncoming troops who were meant to liberate the city. I was fired with enthusiasm and asked to be able to go and help with the building but of course was refused, being told I was far too young. How come I was old enough for some things and too young for other things? I would never be able to understand grown-ups. I wanted to be a hero and save the city from destruction.

When next in the flat, searching for food, I again peered out of the window, narrowly missing a sniper's bullet and saw the pavements outside our house had been torn up and used to build the barricades. I still wished I was old enough to help, but other tasks had to be completed and, anyway, my mother needed me.

After nearly a week, when we thought most of the fighting was over, we were allowed to go back up to our flats. My mother had the forethought to pack all her jewellery, by giving the most important pieces to me to put in my shoes. Other pieces she hid in the baby's pram, and money she gave to my cousin to hide in his shoes. Hastily, we packed more necessary clothing and items of food for my baby sister. We had hardly finished, when there was a loud knock on the door, and armed soldiers stood there shouting abuse at us and said they were to escort or shove us downstairs into waiting lorries. The caretaker, a Czech begged for leniency for my mother, saying that she was never any trouble and that she was a good person. The young, eager soldiers answered that the only good German was a dead one and led us away.

We were herded onto lorries with other German residents. Some tried to avoid capture and were beaten to a pulp in front of us and then thrown into the vehicle, bleeding profusely. Slowly, our lorry drove off, accompanied by jeering and swearing and the throwing of stones. We had no idea of where we were going and clung together in fear. At last, we arrived at some sort of disused cinema, where we were unloaded like cattle and herded into the semi-dark, cold building. We stayed there all night, cowering and trying to sleep, while all around us people were moaning and crying. Those who had been beaten until their heads resembled a blood orange were actually dying all around us.

My cousin and I were terrified, never having seen or heard of such atrocities. It seemed a very long night with fear hanging over us like a heavy, suffocating blanket.

The next morning, more young, enthusiastic soldiers, both Czech and Russian, appeared and began to line us up, saying they had orders to shoot us. After brandishing their rifles and firing some shots over our heads, they started laughing and began a strip search, to see what treasures and jewellery we were hiding. They particularly enjoyed searching the women, who were given no privacy and often stripped naked. There was more laughter and jeering from the soldiers. My mother was lucky to have only to succumb to hand searching and delving into her bosom and in her pants. I held my breath knowing that I carried the family jewels, but I was not searched. Neither was my cousin. The baby, too, was left sleeping undisturbed. The soldiers had too much fun molesting the women and beating the men and thus paid no notice to us children.

After they had their fun, we were then bundled onto another lorry and driven to yet another place where we were kept for the next week. It was a disused school building, so we had more space and proper toilets. Other Germans from the nearby vicinity were brought there, too, in other cattle trucks.

The school was a huge building with many rooms that we all had to share. There must have been at least fifty or more people. I never met them all. At least there was running cold water as well as the toilets. We were left lying around and were fed on watery slops. Next to our building, Russian soldiers were housed, and whenever I went into the yard to hang up my sister's nappies—by special permission of course—I could smell the lovely, tantalizing cooking fumes from their kitchen. The young soldiers chatted to me, and as Czech is very similar to Russian, I could converse quite well with them. The rest was done in sign language. They were kind and very sorry for me, so they told me to bring a bucket and cover it with the nappies, so that they could give me some of their leftover food. Gladly, I complied and rushed upstairs to 'hang' up some more nappies and then handed the bucket over to the waiting soldiers. This became a regular feature, and we could enjoy a little nourishing food, such as chicken soup, goulash stew, and other leftovers that we shared with others in our room. The young Russian soldiers always looked out for me and after chatting in a friendly manner plied me with more food. We all were very grateful to the kind souls especially as we were shown no kindness by anyone else. I became quite the heroine.

One day, after more body searching and shooting bullets above our heads, we were once more herded onto lorries and driven off into the country outside Prague to a village called Barsht, where we were deposited in order to be housed on a large farm that had previously been used by the Germans as a labour camp. Now it was our turn to be in a labour camp, having to suffer the same indignities as had before us the Czech, Russian and even Jewish prisoners.

The building was large and rectangular with an open space in the middle—a rather large quadrangle, with stables on all sides and watchtowers at each corner. Above the stables was the accommodation for the soldiers. We were all allocated a stable, with nothing in it but straw and told to make that our home for the foreseeable future.

Cold water and primitive toilets were the only provisions available. Food would be provided once a day, only after a day's work in the fields had been accomplished by the prisoners.

Thankfully, we fell asleep in the warm straw, only to be woken at 5.00 a.m. for roll call. Everyone was assigned their work detail for the day. However, before work, soldiers came with scissors and razors to cut off all the women's hair. There was much crying and pleading and once the soldiers had had their fun, they ceased their bizarre play, and thus, luckily, my mother escaped that particular humiliation. Everyone was then marched out of the camp to start the day's labour. I was told to mind my sister and that my cousin and I had to stay close all day.

Work in the fields from dawn to dusk became the everyday occurrence for everyone. Some people were told that they were not pulling their weight, for as they were professional and academic people, unused to such jobs, found the work very difficult and exhausting. They were beaten unmercifully and many died of their injuries.

The soldiers soon discovered that I was fluent in Czech and would use me in order to send me on errands outside the camp, while my cousin looked after the baby. As the gates to the camp opened, I was often stoned, and sworn at by the villagers and their children, until I shouted back similar obscenities in Czech and then they left me in peace to complete my given tasks of running the soldiers' errands. The inhabitants of the village soon became used to seeing me outside the gates of the prison camp and left me in peace to what I had to do.

Performing tasks for the soldiers had a rewarding side for me, as sometimes I would get some extra food or sweets that I shared with my cousin. I was also able to overhear any plans the soldiers made in order to make life difficult for the prisoners, and I could therefore warn everyone of what was being planned.

One day one of the prisoners had died, and the soldiers found a gold watch on his dead body, so they immediately started another search in case others had managed to hide things away. I was upstairs in the guardroom, performing one of my tasks, when I heard of the proposed search. All the prisoners were out in the field, so I could not warn anyone. I rushed down as soon as I could and hid my mother's jewellery by making a hole in the pram mattress, stitching it up, and then putting my baby sister to sleep on it. I wheeled her up and down while she screamed, not wanting to sleep, but in the end she tired herself out crying and fell asleep. When the soldiers came to search the pram, I dared them to wake her, as they must have heard her endless crying beforehand, so they left. My cousin and I soon got used to the life and adapted best we could.

One morning, when we woke, we were horrified to see that our clothes had a life of their own, as they were literally walking away from us. We were alive with lice, and they were everywhere, in our clothes as well as in our hair.

We did have to laugh at our walking garments, but we soon stopped as we received a scrubbing in cold water, from my mother and were doused in paraffin in order to kill all the creepy crawlies.

Thank goodness we were not set alight!

My mother kept her nose clean and did as she was told. Being a lovely woman, in her prime, she attracted much attention from the soldiers.

I woke up one night to hear my mother laughingly plead to retrieve her panties that a soldier tried to get off her. I immediately cried out that I had a nightmare and the luckless soldier ceased his amorous game. However, he did not give up easily and often sought out my mother's attention. He tried to bring in food and make her lot a little easier. My mother in turn enjoyed the attention she was receiving and as it benefited us all, she did not feel like a traitor. Anyway, the soldier was kind and generous and a good human being.

Days went into weeks, the harvest was gathered and the long days became shorter workdays.

CHAPTER 8

ONE DAY, I WAS CALLED up to the guard room, as I thought for some errands, but when I got there, a gentleman stood before me and I was asked whether I knew this man. One look and I knew but said 'no'. I felt as if I was St Peter betraying Jesus and denying all knowledge of who he was. I felt terrible and did not know what to do for the man before me was my father, who had traced me through the Red Cross and had at last found his beloved daughter—me.

Speechless, I waited for my mother to be called and tell me what to do. I was not supposed to mention my father, and here he was in the flesh. I was in real anguish. After much discussion and the showing of legal papers, I was told that I had to go with my father as I now was a free citizen. I was Czech and Jewish, thus not to be connected with the German Arian race.

Like it or not, I had to leave.

Sadly, I left the camp behind me and promised my mother that I would soon, somehow or other, set them free. I felt guilty and responsible for my mother, sister, and cousin. I had no choice but to go with my father.

My father and I left to go back to Prague, where he lived with a former girlfriend, who had a one-bedroom flat in the basement of a large apartment block in the centre of town in one of the many beautiful squares.

I was allocated the couch in the kitchen to sleep on. My father adored me and spoiled me as often as he could considering the poor circumstances we were living under I remember waking one night and saying that I was hungry, so my father set to and baked me some latkes (Jewish potato cakes or pancakes), which I ate as a midnight feast. Another time, it was toasted bread with garlic rubbed on—delicious!

My father was always ready to spoil me. We had great fun together, singing songs from the old shows and dancing around the parks. I went out shopping with him and helped him when out and about as he did not speak Czech but only German, and that was not appropriate at that time. Slavka, his lady friend, was there but kept a low profile.

I did not forget my promise to my mother, saying I would set her free and so started upon my quest. First, I asked my father all about my mother's life history, wrote it down, and learnt it by heart. Then, I set out for the nearest police station to ask advice and to find out what I had to do. They told me that they could not help me as they were just ordinary policemen and gave me the address of the military police. So I went and found their headquarters, asked to see a man in charge, and proceeded to recite my mother's story. I said she was born in Poland and therefore was not German, so please release her from prison. The solder's were very amused to see a little girl of nine years old pleading so earnestly on her mother's behalf and therefore tried to help me by sending me to another office where there were more important officers of higher rank. I repeated my story all over again. They listened politely but said they could not help me. Try another office, where the elite officers of a higher echelon were based. My father could not come with me due to his language difficulties, and he did not want to upset any of the authorities. He did, however, give me a lot of encouragement and advice.

Unperturbed, I went from one office to another, each time getting to see men in higher office, until at last I was sent to a palace where I was told they may be able to help me.

Prague had many beautiful palaces, which were now being used as head offices for politicians and high-ranking personnel.

I found this particular palace, a very ornate, baroque place, and entered the portals, enquiring where I had to go. Being shown along many lavish passages and through halls that looked more like the mirror room in Versailles, I was at last left outside huge double doors and told to knock and wait. A voice boomed out 'come in', and I entered a vast, splendid room. I had to walk, what seemed like kilometres in order to reach the baroque desk, behind which a stern-looking gentleman sat. My nose just about reached over the desk, but this did not put me off. In a clear voice, I started once again to plead my mother's cause. At last, after much amusement on his part, he called other officials who, too, were bemused by the small girl speaking and pleading so fearlessly and eloquently on behalf of her mother, that at last they produced release papers for my mother, baby sister, and cousin.

Triumphantly, I returned home to my father and asked if I could collect my family. My father and his lady discussed the situation and told me that I could go and get them the next day. Eagerly, I waited the time and then travelled to the familiar camp in order to get their release. I was welcomed by everyone, and even the guards had smiles and cheerful words for me. Released at last, we all returned to Prague that day, and my mother was told she could, for the time being stay in the one bed roomed apartment with my father and his partner. They slept in the sitting room, and I continued to sleep in the kitchen. To me it all seemed a perfect arrangement, but it must have been very strange for Slavka, whose apartment it was.

My mother still had all her jewellery that I had carried so uncomfortably in my shoes, but the money that had been given to my cousin for safe keeping was a little ruined. He too had hidden it in his shoes, and his sweaty feet, had caused some damage. At least my mother did not feel quite as penniless as she had been and could contribute a little toward the household.

A week passed, and my mother recovered her strength. After much discussion with my father, she said she had to go to a transit camp in order to be repatriated with her family in Germany. I was not very happy, but my mother explained that she needed to start a new life and therefore needed the support of her sisters and mother. She also needed to return my cousin to his mother, who must surely be worried about him.

She had inquired about procedures and ways to get to Germany. She was told she had to go via a transit camp.

Thus, one day, with much hugging and crying, they all said goodbye and travelled to Pilsen where the transit camp was. She had been promised a speedy date of departure to Germany. I promised them that I would visit as soon as they were settled.

While I was waiting to visit my mother in the camp, I asked my father if I could go and see some old friends, who were still living in Prague. I had a plan. I went from one family to another, asking for food, money, or clothing for my mother and sister.

Everybody gave me something, as they were all very fond of my mother. I collected food, money, and clothing in a small suitcase. I even went to visit the soldier from the camp, who had fancied my mother, and he gave me fresh farm food to take to them. Now fully prepared, I left the suitcase with a friend and asked my father's permission to go and see my girlfriend and stay a few nights with her. I felt really bad to have to lie to my father who had been so good and understanding at all times, but my mother had written that there was a scarlet fever outbreak at the camp and I did not think my father would let me go there. I had already had scarlet fever, so I was not worried about catching the disease. I went to the familiar station in Prague and checked out which train I had to catch in order to travel to Plzen. Taking the first available through train and clutching my well-filled suitcase, I then travelled to Pilsen.

On arrival, I asked for directions, and when I at last found the camp, the guards would not let me in as visitor's time was over. No matter how hard I cried, they would not relent. I asked for the nearest police station and went there explaining my situation. I asked where I could sleep for the night, as I knew no one in the area. They took me to a shelter for homeless men. It was a large, derelict-looking building with many rooms, and there I was given a bed in a corner of the large dormitory full of vagrants. I was really too frightened to sleep with a lot of old men, who coughed and spluttered throughout the night. Terrified or not, there was no one to comfort me, so I curled up on the hard bed with no sheets—just a grubby pillow and a rough blanket—and held my case tightly all night. I hoped I would not be murdered in my sleep.

Somehow, the night passed and I was safe. I remembered the way back to the camp, although the city was strange to me. I went straight back to the camp, which was a large, enclosed area of Nissen huts, surrounded by a big and very high wall with guards at various strategic places. A different guard was on duty and being full of compassion, let me in to see my mother. She was delighted with all the 'goodies' and we all spent a happy day together.

I thought I had a problem with my female parts and as I could not share this with my father, was glad when my mother investigated and reassured me that all was well and normal and that I was just growing up.

I played with my baby sister and dressed her in her new dresses that I brought her. My cousin and I also had time to share special moments together. The day passed too quickly and I was supposed to leave at a certain time. When guards came to check, I hid in the toilet and thus was able to spend the night and another day with my family.

There were more sad goodbyes the next day and promises of an early return.

I arrived safely back at my father's place, saying I had a great time. No questions were asked and I did not want to talk about things as I still felt guilty for the deceit and all the lies I had told.

Being of school age, I had to attend a Czech school, where I learned Russian amongst other subjects. I liked school, had excellent reports, and soon made many friends. My best friend was a girl my age named Bozenka, and we had great fun together.

One day, I asked whether I could go ice-skating with my new friend Bozenka. My father was not too keen but relented, not wanting to disappoint me. He warned me to take care and not to break a limb. Wow, I did fall and hurt my hand. Having said that I would be very careful, I did not want to go home until I had been to a hospital to check it out. I found a hospital with a casualty ward and explained that my father could not come with me and told doctor what had happened. He said I had broken my arm and went about setting the bone, which was very painful. I had no anaesthetic, but had to sit on a stool and two doctors just pulled and pulled to get the bone back into place in order to straighten the arm. My doctor then proceeded to put the arm into plaster. Feeling very foolish, I went home to my father, and explained. I thought he would be angry, but he just hugged me.

The following weekend, I asked to go and visit my mother and my father gave me the fare and plenty of advice and instructions. Once more I set off for Pilsen, and this time was allowed in. Again I stayed the night with my mother and travelled back the next day. I was heartbroken to have to leave them all over again, and said I would return soon.

How was I to know that this was the last time for many years to come before I would see them all again, At last, they all left to travel to Germany and were reunited with the family in Pegnitz.

I returned home to my father, and life went on in a by now familiar pattern. I went to school, went skating, or just played in the park with my friends, and my father continued to spoil me in every way, despite the severe rationing not only of food but also of clothes. My father and I had a lot of fun, and I felt loved, adored, and spoiled. He never talked about the war years or of what had happened to him.

Years later, I found out that he had been taken to a concentration camp called Terezin or Theresian Stadt. This concentration camp was the flagship of the Nazis. It contained many musicians, artists, and actors and was shown off to visiting inspection teams as the sort of concentration camps the Germans organized. The rumours of atrocities carried out in other camps were thus hopefully squashed. My father managed to survive by turning his hand to mending shoes. Being a cobbler was very important as everyone needed shoes of sorts, especially in the very cold winters. He also helped with the theatrical productions and concerts to entertain important visitors to the camp.

All this I never knew at the time and could never ask him about at a later date, when I was old enough, as he had died by then and the many, many questions and ideas that I would have liked to share with him were no longer possible.

One day, my father informed me that he had received a letter from his niece in England and it had been suggested that I fly out to stay with her. I had never heard of her because she belonged to my father's side of the family and was older than my mother. I refused to even contemplate such a journey and did not wish to part from my newly found father. I loved him passionately.

However, I was persuaded that this was for the best, and I could always return if things did not work out. My father told me of all the wonderful opportunities that would be available to me in England and that it would make him and my mother very proud if I would avail myself of them. Always ready for a new adventure, I decided to give it a go and cross the North Sea to the far distant, misty land that was England. Did not princes and princesses have to go and start life in strange countries? So I, too, would be like a princess and seek out a new promised land.

Once again I had to go and visit all the bureaucratic offices as my father did not speak Czech. This time, I was sent to an office called UNRA—United Nations Relief Association—(nowadays known as UNICEF), which was situated in a very modern building in the centre of town. Everyone there was very welcoming and received me with great understanding. They assured me that they would complete all the necessary paper work, get me a passport, as well as arrange for a flight by aeroplane out to England. I had to visit their office several times, and at each visit was welcomed and spoiled with sweets or chocolate—unknown to us in Prague. At last, all formalities were completed, and I went to collect the paper work. I had a Stateless Passport as I could not prove any nationality. That did not worry me at all; I knew who I was. As I left the offices, the smiling staff waved me goodbye and said that the King and Queen of England were waiting for me. I laughed and retorted that Kings and Queens were only found in storybooks and did not exist. Still chuckling, I went home to tell all the news to my father and show him all the official paper work.

It was a sad time, for once again I had to say goodbye to people I loved, especially my father who was such a wonderful man. He reassured me that all would work out really well and that I would be very happy in England. Before journeying so far, he sent me to church to see the priest and get his blessing and have special prayers said to keep me safe so far from home.

Before I left Prague, I wanted to go to visit the lovely flat where my mother and I had been so happy. I took a tram and fearfully entered the apartment block, remembering the violent times when we were driven out of our home under gunfire. I was afraid someone would recognize me. I took courage into my hands and biting my lip I climbed the stairs to the second floor and knocked on the door of the flat. A lady answered, and I haltingly explained that I used to live there and wondered if she still had any toys, photos, or mementoes that I could have. Sadly, she replied that all was thrown away, but she thought there might still be a photo album with some photographs around the place. She was very kind and understanding. She invited me in, and I stayed in the hallway and I shut my eyes, not wanting to remember too much of our home. In my mind I saw the place as it used to be and heard the familiar voices around me—my baby sister gurgling, my mother singing and laughing, and my cousin joking. This made me open my eyes, but everything looked so different now, which made me sad.

The lady returned shortly and very apologetically handed me my mother's photo album with only a few photos intact. She was sorry that so many photos were missing and that there was nothing else to give me. She wished me well, and I said my thanks and goodbyes. Clutching the precious album and with tears smarting my eyes, I went back home to my father.

At last all tasks were completed. I had packed my meagre belongings, and my father took me to the airport. I had never flown before or indeed even seen an aeroplane, so I was very excited, which took away some of my sadness at leaving him and my beautiful Prague. Indeed, I even had no time to worry about the unknown person I was about to meet in a strange country where they spoke a completely different language. Crying for my father and waving madly, I boarded the plane and was welcomed by the cabin staff who said that they would look after me on the journey and hand me over to my cousin Resi once we arrived in England. I continued waving goodbye to my father and shouted my promise to write lengthy letters telling him all about my new life and the new adventures that lay ahead.

How was I to know then that I would never see him again, as he was already ill with cancer of the larynx and would die within a few years?

Why, oh why was life so cruel?

Every time that I was loved by someone, I was sent away into the great unknown, never to see their beloved face again. I was only ten years old.

Chapter 9

I sat in the aeroplane, a miserable, little hunched figure, crying as if my heart would break. The stewardess and crew tried hard to cheer me up, but I was too miserable as now I had been parted not only from my beloved mother but also from my newly found father who adored me. I just sat there while waves of misery engulfed me. As I had a window seat, I began, after a while to look out of the window and was amazed to see the world spread beneath us like a huge toy with tiny houses, little forests, and even little mountains. Rivers sparkled in the sunshine like long ribbons spread across the landscape. Above us the sky was clear blue, except for the occasional cotton-wool cloud drifting by. My sadness had not abated, but I became interested in my surroundings, both outside as well as inside the plane. Although I had never been inside an aeroplane, I found it most uninteresting. The plane was a very primitive and uncomfortable affair—nothing like the ones we have today. I was not really aware of the other passengers and kept myself to myself, watching the world go by beneath us.

By then, I had stopped crying but still felt incredibly sad. Suddenly, I developed an overwhelming earache and was unable to hear anything. I called the cabin staff and explained my predicament and they tried to explain that it was caused by the cabin as the plane was not properly pressurized. I could not hear what they said, but felt reassured by their presence and presumed that all was a normal procedure. By now I felt really cut off from everyone and although I saw their kindness and concern, felt very much on my own. I had lost my hearing and was quite deaf. What was to happen to me next?

The short flight continued uneventfully, and before long we were descending and I was shown the white cliffs of Dover and the seven sisters that were for me the beginning of a strange new land. It did not take long for us to land in Croydon—or was it Northolt, outside London? I cannot remember, and there is no one who can tell me. Not that it made the slightest difference to me what the place was called, as all was strange and foreign to me. The airport seemed small, with just one or two buildings.

Someone took my hand and led me outside the plane and into the airport building where two ladies stood who seemed to be expecting me. They had a photograph of me that my father had sent them, but I had no idea of what my cousin looked like, except that she was a year older than my mother.

They came toward me and embraced me, welcoming me to England. I just smiled as I could not hear anything they said. The stewardess explained to them my momentary deafness that would disappear shortly. Somehow my luggage arrived and formalities were seen to, as I just stood in my silent world, gazing about me.

I was led to a waiting bus that took us into London where we boarded a train. Looking out of the window, I found London huge and sprawling and was quite unimpressed by the houses which all looked the same and the busy shopping roads full of drab people. Oh, where was my lovely Prague with its tall elegant houses and broad, tree-lined avenues?

The short train journey took us into the middle of Reading where busses waited for arriving passengers. I was used to trams and thought the busses very strange vehicles. They were dark red and had spaces on top. I had never seen a double-decker bus before and was fascinated. I wanted to go onto the top deck but as we had luggage we had stay below. By now I had had plenty of time to study my two companions. One was short and plump—that was my cousin Resi, while the other one, whom I was to call Aunty Gizi, was slim and tall. They both smiled a lot and seemed as nervous as I was and did not really know how to talk to me. Luckily they both spoke German. They were both Jewish and had fled Hitler's regime and arrived as refugees some years ago. My cousin was from Berlin and Aunt Gizi from Vienna. My hearing had returned a little, so that I did not feel quite so isolated and tried to chat to them, telling them news of my father. I had to speak very quietly as it was deemed wrong to speak German in England so soon after the war.

Suddenly, we arrived at our final destination in the suburb of Reading. We got off the bus and walked just a little way to where my new home was to be. I was amazed to see a row of houses all looking exactly alike, with small manicured front gardens.

They were all semi-detached houses and had they been tiny, would look like toy town houses, to be played with. I was led into one of these houses and was told that Resi and Gizi rented that house and I was to live with them there. A room had been prepared for me, overlooking the garden. It was a lovely, bright, and comfortable room and someone (I later found out it was Gizi) had put a doll on the bed and toy animal ornaments on the windowsill. The windows were not double-glazed and neither did they have two windows together to keep out the cold, as we had at home. There was no heating in the bedrooms and only open fires downstairs to keep us warm. Oh, I had to tell both my mother and father about this toy town house and would write them each a long letter. However, that night I fell exhausted into sleep as so much had happened and there was so much to learn.

The next few days passed in a haze. I was shown around the town and the neighbourhood and spent much time with Aunty Gizi who had far more patience than Resi and was tireless in explaining everything to me. I remember shocking my cousin one day when I went upstairs and washed my hair, as it needed attention. I was well and truly told off and called irresponsible, as I now would catch cold. I really did not understand all the fuss that followed, as I had always been a very independent child and had to learn early on to look after myself. I was told I had to be taken in hand. I was not allowed to wear my white knee socks as they smacked of German Hitler Youth. Neither was I allowed to keep my Shirley Temple curls, but had my hair brushed out and put into tight plats. My aunt Gizi softened the blow by buying me some lovely colourful ribbons with which to adorn myself. I also went shopping with her to buy some clothes as befit an English child. She even took me to see a film at the local cinema (*Random Harvest*) as I missed seeing films. I was quite impressed with the film but could not understand a word of it as I spoke no English.

I found all the food in England very bland and badly cooked. Everything tasted watery and not as good as my grandmother's, mother's, or my father's cooking. They had all been excellent cooks and could make a feast with the poorest ingredients.

My poor cousin Resi! She had never been used to children, as she had been an opera singer and used to theatre life. She felt very responsible for me and wanted to do her best for me but had no idea of how to even start looking after a child. I certainly did not fit into any mould that she thought of as a child. She did not want to let my father down and was really worried as to what to do with me. Both Gizi and Resi went out to work all and every day (except Sundays), so what was to happen to me?

Resi and Gizi went to seek help from the Jewish Board of Guardians and begged them to help. They suggested that I be sent to a hostel for working girls in Reading, which was run by two ladies from Berlin. Thus, it came about that I came to live in the hostel and was by far the youngest girl in the home. The other eight girls had been brought to England on the Kinder Transport (Children's Train), which collected children from all over Europe where Hitler was persecuting Jews. They came from Germany, Austria, Hungary, and Poland. They had been in England some time and were now training to take up jobs in various fields and living together in the hostel. One by one they left shortly after my arrival, and newcomers to the hostel were then much younger than I. The children were from Jewish families who could no longer look after them and the Jewish Board of Guardians took over their care and responsibility. There were about ten of us living at the hostel under the care of Hilde and Sophie, the two ladies from Berlin. Sophie had been a geography teacher and Hilde a nursery worker, and it had been their dream to run a home for children instead of the older working girls. I shared a room with a girl, Hedy, who was a year younger. The other boys and girls shared separate rooms.

The hostel was a large, detached house in the leafy part of Reading, beautifully situated and yet still quite central to the middle of town. It had a large garden surrounding it and was not overlooked by any other house.

I took this move in my stride as I could see the predicament Gizi and Resi were in, having me thrust into their home. I was told they would keep my room for me so that I could come and visit at weekends. This however did not happen, although I would spend the odd Sunday with them.

I had no difficulty in settling into the hostel. Sophie would teach me English every day, and I soon became fluent enough to be able to converse with people. I learnt how to say w instead of v, as in water and how to master the 'th'. Sophie made up a rhyme: 'Why, which, when, what, would whether 'cause Sophie taught me how; and how to say th's—and how to say th's in this, and that and things.'

Then it was time for me to continue my education and as I had attended a grammar school in Prague, Hilde and Sophie sought the help of Professor Morley, who lived in Reading and had an oversight of what was happening at the hostel. She managed to get me an interview at the local grammar school for girls, called Kendrick Girls' School, where Miss Towne, the headmistress, accepted me into the school on a trial basis. Duly, I was given the school uniform, a navy tunic, white blouse, and a red and black striped tie, and of course the Beret and a blazer, both with the school badge on it. I felt like a million dollars and felt that at last I belonged somewhere. It was only years later that I discovered that the uniform was paid for by the English teacher at the school, a Miss Appleby. Not knowing this, I did not feel like a charity case but loved being at school and could hardly wait for each day that I could attend.

I was put into the first year that was in fact the year below the one I was supposed to be in, but as I spoke very little English it was thought best for me to be with the younger pupils. While the others had normal lessons, I was sat in a corner and made to read Beatrix Potter books and translate and write stories about them. Thus I became competent in the English language and soon was able to join the rest of the class in their studies. Sophie continued to help me at home so that soon I was able to sit the same exams as my classmates and to my surprise came out with top marks. I was now able to jump a year and be put with my age group. It was a lovely class and I made many friends, particularly a girl name Ann and another named Janet. The three of us were inseparable. We worked and played together and vied to be at the top of the class in all subjects, which we always were.

Life was very strange though, as now I was not allowed to speak of my German past, my Catholic upbringing, or my family in Germany. Now I was a Jewish refugee (the dreaded word 'Jew' that I once had to hide and deny!). Once again, I had to belie my past and keep all a big secret. I therefore put everything to the back of my mind, and my only wish was to be accepted, loved, and be the same as everyone else.

Life at school was great, and although I had no loving family to go home to, I became a staunch member of the grammar school and wore the uniform with pride. I joined the choir, and when the opportunity arose to learn a musical instrument, Hilde and Sophie decided on my behalf that I should learn the cello, as I was a big, strapping girl and could manage to carry the instrument around. That seemed a silly reason to me, but I did not mind which instrument I learnt. So I started cello lessons with a Miss Plunket. I loved the mellow tones of the cello and made fast progress and soon joined the school orchestra. However, I was lazy when it came to practising at home and would have been a far better player had I heeded my teacher's words. This I now regret whole heartedly.

My two friends also joined the choir and orchestra, and we had great times giving concerts. I loved all my music lessons, were they practical or theory. This was enhanced by the fact that I had a 'pash' or crush, on my music teacher, Miss Dankworth (sister of Johnny Dankworth as I was to discover later). I adored the lady and went out of my way to bump into her at every possible occasion. When she left the school, I transferred my hero worship to her successor, Miss Timmins. She was quite a different character and quite shy, which went well with her name. All my dreams and fantasies were about these two ladies, perhaps even more poignant as I so wanted to be loved by someone and have them for myself, instead of having to share Hilde and Sophie with ten other children.

My favourite lesson, apart from music, was English, as Miss Appleby made English literature come alive, and Shakespeare, Milton, Shaw, Austin, and

Bronte became my favourite bedtime companions, as well as many others writers that she had introduced us to.

When I was fourteen years old, I was offered the job of science monitor, which meant coming to school early in the morning and setting up equipment in the science laboratories and then staying after school to clean and put everything away. I loved all these tasks, and even better, I received a small payment for performing the work.

I enjoyed all lessons at school, such as science, art, history, and geography, but mathematics I could not master enough to be proficient in the subject. Sports—well the less said the better. I was a big girl with a well-developed bust, which was embarrassing as it wobbled when running or bounced up and down uncontrollably when having to jump or skip. I was always told by Hilde and Sophie that I was fat, thus I found physical education hard to compete in. When we learnt tennis, there were visiting pupils from abroad and I was told to help them and see to their wellbeing, so I got behind in the sport and found my hand and eye co-ordination to be too poor to play with my friends, who by then wanted a good game. Sad but true. However swimming made up for the lack of competency in other sports. Having learnt to swim with my cousin in Bavaria, I was not afraid of water and would greatly enjoy the swimming lessons at the local baths.

As I got older, I took a great interest in my religious studies and started to read about all sorts of religions. At home I compared these religions and marvelled at the conflict that always arose in the name of religion. Was not God the same God for everyone, no matter what name He was given? I took to talking to the religious instruction teacher and she provided me with many books to read. She was a Quaker—a member of the Society of Friends. I joined her at many meetings and became fascinated by this sect. Why should we all repeat the mumbo jumbo that is laid down by the different churches? Why perform the almost dramatic rites set out by churches? I found it easy to speak to God in my own words and be moved by the spirit to sing or quote poetry. After a year or so, I started to question the way of life of the Quakers too and thought that many people only speak during a meeting because they are full of themselves and not because the spirit had moved them. I stopped going to the meetings but continued to try and find a religion that would satisfy my needs. I sorely needed to believe in something and missed my Catholic upbringing, with the saints and the angels who were always there to protect and comfort me.

At that time, school was everything to me and I revelled in the academic life. I still had my childhood dream to become a doctor—a paediatrician—and so made sure that I stayed at the top of the class in all my studies. I got on well with all the teachers and with all my peers and was quite a popular figure at school.

My flying dreams continued all through the years, and as time passed, I became more adept in my skill and could soar ever higher. I no longer had to fly down a stairway, but could now stand on a windowsill, spread my arms like the wings of a bird and then leap out and fly. To get higher into the sky, I would make swimming movements—like those when doing the breaststroke and thus reach heights well above the land below and keeping clear of all the high trees. It was a wonderful feeling to be soaring high in the air, swooping down and then reach even higher. Sometimes, I would turn on my back and just float, enjoying the caressing air or when flying at night, admire the stars and the moon. I loved this feeling of freedom and always woke up happy.

One night, I dreamed that I was pursued by something evil and flew higher and higher trying to get away from this frightening feeling. I was terrified and in a frenzy to escape. I flew into the hostel house, up the stairs, and heard a voice calling me: 'Do not be afraid. You are safe. Come up into the attic.'

As I flew up the stair, I heard children's voices singing, 'Praise him, praise him all the little children. He is love . . .' I arrived at the attic door and sat down. I could not get into the attic but was told that GOD is there and I would be well looked after. I felt such peace and awe steal over me and to this day remember that wonderful feeling. Whenever I was unhappy, I would remember that dream and felt comforted.

I hated weekends and holidays when I could not go to school and be with my friends, and dreaded the time when I would have to leave school.

I had done well in my School Certificate—GCSE—and passed all my eleven subjects, two at pass level and all the others with credits. I received matriculation exemption, which would make it easy for me to get to university. I wanted to go into the sixth form, but Hilde and Sophie, who were by now my guardians, would not allow it. I should go and learn a job and earn my keep. Neither I nor my teachers or head teacher could persuade them otherwise.

I had to go back again to my life at the hostel or children's home as it was now renamed. I was the oldest one in the family group and therefore was expected to help at all times with the housework, washing, cooking, and care of the younger children. Everyone had a rota of work to be carried out according to age. Every day, I had to sweep the stairs and the hall and help with the preparation of high tea.

To my shock and horror, Hilde and Sophie were vegetarians, and all of us had to follow suit. Where, oh where were my sausages, salamis, and roast dinners? I was a great carnivore and sadly missed the lack of meat. Oh, there were other new treats such as dried bananas, tartex—a vegetarian pate—and freshly baked cheesecake. As we were in the post-war years, food rationing was still around and there were great shortages. We had only powdered, dried eggs. Vegetables were plentiful, so we never went hungry. As time passed things became easier and more food was made available. Sweet rationing however continued for quite a time, and I always saved up all my coupons to have a real treat. I loved chocolate, became hooked, and am a chocoholic to this day.

For high tea I had learnt how to bake brown, whole-meal bread and make cakes and biscuits. When we sat down to eat, Hilde and Sophie would always point out that I was too fat and had to eat sparingly. I was not as slim and good-looking as Hedy. They always compared me with her. I liked her and we got on well together. She too had lost touch with her parents and was fostered eventually by a Swiss family. I really missed her when she left, as then there were only much younger children and there was no one with whom I could emphasize.

I always ate everything that was on my plate, not even leaving a crumb, even if I did not like the food that I was given. Being told I was fat, I was given Ryvita instead of bread and small helpings of cakes. As a result I would always ogle as to which were the largest and biggest pieces on offer and make a bid for them—even if I was told off and made to feel ugly and ungainly. To this day I still look for the largest portions, much to my shame.

After high tea, I had to wash up and tidy the kitchen and dining room and help put the children to bed before settling down to my homework.

I was in close touch with my mother at all times and would write to her often, telling her all my thoughts and feelings. She too would write and say she missed me. When my birthday came around, she would send me parcels with books and German sausage and salami, as well as German biscuits. She also sent me photographs, and I would hug these to me and cry bitter tears, as I missed being with her and missed Germany, about which I was not allowed to speak. I hid the sausages and ran up to my room, hoarding all my goodies into a safe place. I would not share these with anyone but would sit up in the dark and eat them while hiding under my blanket. Yes, blanket and not my lovely, cosy, feather bed cover, which I missed so much. I found sheets and blankets draughty and uncomfortable and fantasized about my feather beds.

At weekends, I had to hand wash all the children's dirty socks and hankies, which I hated. Then, it fell to me to take all the children to the park and play games with them. Lunch and tea table clearance came next. The evenings were organized for us, and there was little time to do anything on my own.

As everyone was Jewish, Friday night was celebrated with special meals, songs, and readings. We were told all the Jewish bible stories and histories and learnt Hebrew songs for each occasion. Hedy and I were taught the recorder and would be asked to play before all festive meals. We learnt songs, dances, and music to suit all occasions, which I enjoyed greatly.

Each Jewish festival had its own story, and we would be asked to re-enact them. I loved the dressing up and play-acting as it reminded me of home. I did however find it difficult to be thought of as a Jewish child, as I continued feeling that I was Bavarian and a Catholic, but kept these feelings to myself. Earlier in my life, I was never allowed to talk about

Jewish relations with whom I had lost touch, and now I was not allowed to be Catholic and German. Why did I always have to hide my identity?

Who was I really? Would I ever belong somewhere and be *me*?

Occasionally, visitors would come and join special events. They all referred to me as Cinderella, as they saw all the chores that I had to fulfil each and every day. One couple that came to stay invited me to come and spend post-Christmas with them and their family in their beautiful home outside Basingstoke. They were the Newson family who were much involved in national education. It was heaven being part of their household, however short the time. I was taken out shopping and bought some new dresses, and we all went out to eat in a real restaurant—a first for me. It was also the first time that I was taken to a Christmas pantomime, which I found magical. However, the time passed too quickly, and sadly I was soon back at the hostel once more.

Life at the hostel continued in a routine way, disrupted occasionally when I was allowed to invite my best friend Ann Taylor to sleep over. At other times Hilde and Sophie would take me along shopping in Reading, which always culminated in having a cup of coffee at the coffee shop. This was a special occasion, and I was very grateful for my little treat.

My mother and father both wrote regular letters, but I was a bad correspondent and felt guilty for not returning the long descriptive letters that I had promised my father, who missed me greatly. He would write all the news from Prague and even send me parcels of goodies that he had saved up for. Some of these parcels contained shoes that he had great trouble in obtaining. I think his experiences in the concentration camp had made him very aware of how important shoes were to human beings. Sadly, by the time they arrived, they did not fit, and I never had the heart to tell him. Another time he sent me photos of himself and Slavka, whom he had married, to make an 'honest' woman of her, so that she would have no difficulties in the eyes of others. My letters, alas, were far and few between, and I always felt guilty that I did not correspond more with him.

In the school holidays Hilde and Sophie would find work for me in order to earn some pocket money. Often I worked in market gardens, picking fruit. That was good fun as I could eat as much as I picked, and I enjoyed the open-air life and the change of being away from the hostel, which I began to hate.

Another time, I was sent to a local doctor's family—the Lattos, who lived in a great house in Caversham. They had three children, two boys and a girl. It was my task to be a sort of mother's helper and work alongside of Mrs Latto, helping with housework and cooking. I also had to take care of the children who were between eight and twelve years old. Doctor Latto was a Naturopathic doctor with a surgery in London as well as in his home. Mrs Barbara Latto (also a doctor, but no longer practicing) was of German origin. I felt very much at home in their family and fitted in very well.

Doctor Latto sometimes had patients staying at his home while on treatment and they slept in garden rooms, specially built for that purpose. Doctor Latto himself mostly slept in the open air, on a proper bed under an open shelter. He would invite me to join him sleeping outside. Thus wrapped in blankets I enjoyed sleeping under the stars that could be seen on three sides. The roof kept us dry, should it rain. I loved the gentle night air caressing my face while the nearby trees whispered lullabies to me.

As I got older, I spend many a holiday helping out at the Latto home, and they became my friends for many years to come.

During one of my working holidays at their home, I was alone in the house, when the front door bell rang. Eagerly I ran to answer, but got a shock when a telegram boy handed me a telegram, briefly stating that my father had died in Prague, having suffered from cancer of the larynx. I shall never forget that dreadful moment of opening the telegram and reading the terrible news. Slowly, I sank onto the floor. Hot tears scalded my cheeks. I was in shock and felt so very guilty for having forgotten my promises to write to him often, telling him everything about my new life out here in England. I was heartbroken, and when Mrs Latto returned, she tried her best to comfort me.

Whenever I received another telegram in years to come, I would break out in a cold sweat and take a very long time in opening the envelope.

Soon life resumed a familiar routine: hostel, school, and working holidays.

One summer, I felt very privileged to be taken on holiday to North Devon by Hilde and Sophie. I thought that perhaps they did like me after all, as for years I had prayed that Sophie would take me under her wing and show me some special love and caring. With hindsight, I think I was only taken on their holiday to keep little Peter, their beloved protégé company.

Sometimes, during the summer holiday, when not working, I was sent to Stoatley Rough Summer School in Haslemere. This was a fantastic treat and I wallowed in the company of other children, whose parents had been refugees and now lived in the UK. Stoatley Rough was a boarding school set in an old mansion with surrounding parkland. There were facilities, such as a swimming pool, tennis courts, and gaming rooms as well as a beautiful library. I really loved the old mansion with its grand, wooden staircase. The school enjoyed a very outgoing, freethinking, and broad outlook in education, valuing the individual and fostering a very caring international environment. I just loved every moment there and could hardly await my next visit there. We were given much freedom, and I enjoyed being able to roam through Haslemere and Hindhead, walk through the heath, past gibbet hill that evoked frightening but thrilling stories of the past. Oh, if only I did not have to return to the hostel, but could become a true Stoatly Roughian and be truly me instead of just a skivvy. Alas the hostel called.

Back at the hostel, I continued my miserable existence, wishing for love and freedom. I was never allowed out in the evening or weekends like other teenagers, but had to report to the minute whenever I went out on errands or when I was allowed to join the Youth Orchestra.

'You are ten minutes late! Where have you been? If you are late again, no more orchestra.'

There were no cinema visits, no concerts to attend, and certainly no boyfriends.

I remember we had a young student of about twenty something come to the hostel to study in the evening, as his digs were cold. Hilde and

Sophie had taken pity on him and welcomed him to work at the hostel in the evening as the children would be in bed. I discovered that he had connections to my music teacher, on whom I had such a crush, so that one evening, after my bath and having completed all chores, I came downstairs to where he was studying in order to question him about my beloved teacher. Hilde and Sophie discovered me talking to him while I was dressed in my nightwear, and I was severely punished and reprimanded. Did I not know that I could become pregnant? (What? By talking?) I never heard the end of that harmless escapade.

Being fifteen years old, I was introduced to Professor Edith Julia Morley in order to be her evening maid. I had met her when I was first sent to the hostel through her kind intervention where school was concerned. She was the first woman professor of English at the University of Reading and was by then well in her fifties or even sixties. She was a very stern and unsmiling paragon of a lady, who expected everything to be just so and demanded a very high standard of service from her maid. I had to go to her house one evening every week, on the maid's day off, and serve her supper. Professor Morley lived in a large, dark house that smelled of age and learning. The kitchen was a huge, austere place, with food and instructions awaiting my arrival. I had to set the table in a most conventional way, with everything in its exact place. A little lectern stood on the table, so that Professor Morley could read while she was dining. Supper had to be served to the exact minute and in complete silence. I was terrified of the old lady, who reminded me of a sort of Miss Haversham, and I therefore made sure that I never made a mistake. For this weekly ritual, I received extra pocket money, as my weekly money received from Hilde and Sophie was about five shillings (twenty-five pence), which did not go very far. That did not really matter as I never had the chance to go out and spend it. So I began to save.

Chapter 10

By the time I was sixteen, I was asked to leave school, and I was devastated. I begged to stay and be allowed to study, but all in vain. My last week at school was a very unhappy one. My friends would stay on in the sixth form and then go to university, while I had to leave. I was enrolled into the Reading Technical College to study and become a nursery nurse. I was inconsolable.

It was at that time that my mother had been given permission to come to England and visit me, being sponsored by Professor Morley. My little sister Sylvia, five years old by then, came with her. They came to stay at the hostel, and although I was delighted to see them, I was torn apart by sadness at leaving my beloved school. My mother could not understand my feelings and thought that I did not care for her. Life was very difficult. I adored my mother and had so often dreamed of being reunited with her, and now that the day had come, I was overcome by sadness. Everyone thought I was uncaring and sullen.

Why did no one understand me?

I must have caused my mother pain by preferring to be at school rather than spend time with her, but every minute was precious to me and I could not tear myself in half, although it felt like it.

I did spend a great deal of time with her, and we talked about everything: my life in England, her life in Germany, and we both wondered what the future would hold for us. My mother related all that had happened since we were last together. She, Schorsch, and baby Sylvia had joined a transport train to Germany, travelling in the cattle trucks. On reaching Bavaria, they were allowed to disembark and were met by my grandmother, who took them all home with her. My cousin was reunited with his mother, and my mother stayed at grandmother's house. They all bought new clothes for my mother and sister, as they had arrived with only the clothes on their backs.

Before long, they were well and truly settled in Bavaria. My mother used this period to search out where her husband, my stepfather, was and eventually traced him. His war record did not amount to much where the German army was concerned. Soon after having to join up, he was taken prisoner of war and transported to the Channel Islands. There he stayed on Alderney Island, where he was able to pursue a musical career of singing and playing the concert piano. He even was able to broadcast. After was he was repatriated to Germany, he arrived with the British army in Iserlohn. Once my mother knew where he was, she travelled with Sylvia to join him, and they settled in Iserlohn where both parents tried to find work and build up a home again.

My stepfather did manual work, and my mother took anything that she could find whenever childcare was available. I was fascinated hearing all this and wished I could have been there with them. On the other hand, I was by now Anglicized and a proper English teenager with new roots in the British Isles. I found that by now I belonged to a group of people in my school and did not want to leave that security. Oh, what was I to do? Why could life not be straightforward?

The time with my mother flew by, and before long, she had to return to Germany. I promised to come to see her as soon as I could get travel papers and find the money to pay for my journey. By that stage, not only was I devastated at having to leave my school but was also heartbroken to have to be parted once again from my mother. We said tearful goodbyes and again promised to write regularly. My mother wished me success with my nursery nurses training and asked me to report my progress.

During all these years spent at the hostel, I had visited Resi and Gizi at various times. Sometimes, we would go on trips or take tea in a restaurant. I could not really get close to Resi and was always on my best behaviour so that she would like me. These visits were infrequent but pleasant nevertheless.

Although I looked forward to my nursery nurses training, I felt that I was like a puppet on a string, being told what to do, when to do it, and what to think. Would I ever find my own identity and be strong enough to tell people what I wanted?

My time at Reading Technical College was about to start, and I found that I had entered yet another stage in my life.

Chapter 11

Reading Technical College was a vast place with a great many students. It did not feel like the cosy, caring atmosphere of my beloved school. However I soon settled into my student life and became a responsible and hardworking member within the nursery nurses department. We had one week in college and the other week at various placements. Subjects studied college included health, biology, first aid, psychology, nutrition, art and craft, needlework, and music. All these disciplines were geared to the care of children between birth and age five. I really enjoyed learning everything that was on offer.

My practical work placements included a day nursery where I had to look after babies and children up to five years olds. The work there was biased towards healthcare and came under the mantle of the Department of Health. Work started at 7.00 a.m. and finished at 6.00 p.m. I had to bath babies and toddlers, prepare their food, and then oversee their eating. I was able to play with all the tiny tots and sometimes take babies for a walk. It was a great learning place, and having had to look after my baby sister before, I found the work easy.

Next, I was placed in a state nursery school with children between the ages of three to five years old. The work there was orientated towards the development and education of young children, and the working day was the same as that in a primary school: 9.00 to 3.30. I had a lot to learn as I had to keep the children occupied and motivated all day long. They all slept for an hour after lunch, when I had to sit with them. I could read while keeping an eye on them but often found it difficult not to fall asleep myself.

I remember having to supervise outdoor play and watched the children as they jumped about on the trampoline, chanting. I thought how happy they were. Suddenly, I was called into the head's office and was asked why I did not stop the children swearing. I said I never heard any bad language and subsequently was asked to listen to their chanting, which consisted of rude swear words that I had never heard of before. The head teacher enlightened me and taught me a few more words so that I could be aware of what the children from the tough estate were saying. I remember being most embarrassed.

I learned how to put out educational equipment, such as puzzles, Legos, and construction toys and had a chance to learn how to use them myself. I was also able to provide creative art materials and help the children to make all sort of colourful creations. The head teacher and nursery teacher and supervisor were all very keen to help me learn everything, and I was an eager student and well respected. They said I could always come back and work there once I finished training and obtained my qualifications.

I was lucky, as I was also sent to a private-training college for nursery nurses that had a maternity home on the premise, a day nursery, and a residential home, thus caring for children from birth to six years old. I absolutely adored that placement as it was so varied in tasks to be completed. I felt competent with all the tasks that I was given, having had the previous placements' experience. My most embarrassing job there was in the maternity home, when I was asked to help while the midwife delivered the baby. I was duly gowned, masked, and scrubbed before entering the labour ward. I had never seen anyone having a baby and just did not know where to look. Thank goodness for the facemask that I had to wear. My face burned, and I tried to look normal, as if I did this sort of thing every day of my life. The birth was so fascinating that I soon forgot my shyness and really assisted the midwife.

Later, I had to nurse the baby and the mother for the next two weeks while they were there. I even had to express breast milk and was once again very glad of having a mask as I felt like giggling, especially as the lady's name was Mrs Brown. The whole procedure reminded me of milking a cow (which I had never done either) and the rhyme 'How now brown cow' kept coming into my mind. However, all was accomplished satisfactorily and Mrs Brown was so pleased with me that she decided to call her baby after me. I was thrilled. My time there passed too quickly. There was so much to learn, and I adored the tiny babies.

My last placement was in a nursery class in a primary school and that gave me great insight of what went on in education—a real school! It was again on a tough housing estate with more language and expressions to learn.

Strangely enough, I have no recollection of other members in my course and did not seem to have made any friends.

During this time, I still lived at the hostel and had my duties and chores to fulfil there as well as my work connected with the college. I still had to look after the children, who of course had grown older too and my tasks therefore had changed. Having learnt to cycle while I was at school so I did not have to pay for buses, I now had to teach the other children how to use their bikes and take them out for cycle runs during the weekend. I still had to cook certain foods, wash up, and do the laundry. How I hated it all. I never felt any closeness with the children, although I liked them. Their names remained a long-lost memory in my mind. I still was not allowed out in the evenings to join friends, and at weekends had more work than ever to do with or without the children. My favourite outing was to the Bluebell Wood, outside Reading. Now that the children had all learnt how to ride bicycles, we could travel further afield and explore the surrounding areas. The Bluebell Wood was magical in the spring, covered by millions of bluebells. The wood was cool and balmy, while the blue carpet of sweet-smelling flowers was reflected in the pond in the midst of this lovely place. I loved the place. My imagination went back to my days in Bavaria, and I could almost hear the bells of the flowers tinkling and calling up the woodland and meadow fairies. Would I never grow up? I hoped not, as I loved my fantasy creatures. We picnicked there in that lovely place before cycling home again.

At this time I was allowed to join the Youth Orchestra, and proudly played m cello there, but did not spend time in practicing the music.

For pocket money I had to continue work at the market garden helping with whatever was growing and had to be done. In winter, however, the work was hard and very cold.

The two years of my training as a nursery nurse passed very fast, and I received honours in my exams and a prize from the technical college for being the best student they had under twenty-one years. Proudly I left and started to look for jobs.

To my great surprise the principal of the Private Nursery Nurses Training College (where I had spent some of my time) rang me up to enquire how I had completed my training and exams and subsequently offered me a job. I was delighted and could not wait to start.

Before taking up my new post, I took my first holiday ever, having saved up enough money, to travel to Germany to visit my mother in Iserlohn. Hilde and Sophie managed to get a travel paper for me, which was a passport for stateless people, as I still appeared to have no nationality, being neither German, Czech, nor British. Full of excitement, I took the train from London, Victoria Station, and set out on my travel. I was so excited to see my mother again, to see my little sister, to see Germany and the way of life that I missed—never mind all those lovely sausages and salami. I was also wondering what my stepfather looked like after all these years.

I was welcomed and made a fuss of, especially by my stepfather. He was such a lovely and gentle man. I loved his voice when he sang and was so proud when he gave concerts. Now at last he could fulfil his ambition of being a musician instead of a boring lawyer. We became great friends. My little sister had grown up and was attending primary school. She was very proud of her cornet full of goodies that she had received on her first school day. I loved her to bits.

Sadly, my mother appeared always critical of me, and I could do little to appease her. Apparently, I looked like a scarecrow and had no dress sense, so she took me shopping so that I could be seen in public and not make her ashamed of me. I was always prompted by her as to how to answer when people enquired after my age. My mother always lied about her age and made herself much younger, so I had to fit in with her. I was often annoyed when being introduced to people as her daughter and they looked at us and asked which was the daughter and which the mother. How could I possibly look old enough at seventeen to be mother to my parent!

My parents lived in a rented one-bedroom flat in the basement of a house. There was no garden, and everything had been sparsely furnished. They worked hard to make things more comfortable, but all seemed a long way removed from the lovely flat that they had in Prague. Their work was physical and not intellectual as their training demanded. My stepfather was always very tired and exhausted. My mother worked at the Rosenthal glass factory, polishing the beautiful crystals and glasses. I was so worried for her as I hated her having to breathe in some of the very fine glass dust. What would it do to her lungs?

As a special treat my mother and stepfather took me to the cinema.

As always when having fun, time passed too quickly, and it was time for me to return to England and start my new job. I promised to return soon and as often as I could.

My new job in the college was a residential position, so I had to move out of the hostel, which delighted me greatly. I was given my own room at the college and donning a nurse's uniform—a navy-blue dress, white apron, and a 'butterfly' headdress—I started my new life as a staff nurse at the Chiltern Nursery Training College. I loved wearing the nurse's uniform as it made me feel that I belonged there.

As I mentioned before, there was a residential nursery, a nursery school where children from outside the college could join us, a residential baby home, and a maternity home. The college was a private training place for about twenty-five students, wanting to become nursery nurses. The college fees were high so that meant that the intake was from well-to-do families. My post as Staff Nurse Daisy involved helping to train students with their practical placements, as well as working full-time within all areas of the college. The principal, Miss Halliday, was a forceful lady and ruled everyone with an iron hand. She informed me during my interview on my first day that Hilde and Sophie had given me a very bad testimonial, saying I was unreliable, lazy, and deceitful, but from what Miss Halliday had seen of me as a student, she did not believe them and wanted to give me a chance to prove myself.

To start off, I was placed in the baby department, where we had about fifteen babies of various ages with a senior staff nurse in charge, who lived in a little room adjoining the babies' rooms. I was in my element looking after these poor little mites that no one wanted. They would hopefully be up for adoption sometime in the future and get loving homes, but in the meantime, there was I, ready to do my best for them and to cuddle and love them. The day was worked in shifts, which included covering night duty as well. I was very happy there but had to move on to the residential home, a Georgian house, set in a vast park like garden. There, children between nine months and six years were placed in small family groups and allocated rooms, which were named after colours. There were six such family groups, and the children stayed together for as long as they were in the residential home. They played, ate, and slept in their room while being cared for by the students in training and supervised by me and another staff nurse, Nurse Marjory, who was older than I. We worked well together and were good friends. The vice-principal, Miss Gardner, an ex-nursing sister, was overall in charge and was a very stern taskmaster, but I really liked her and wanted very much for her to like me. Thus, I worked hard, learnt much, and enjoyed life at the college.

We celebrated all the usual Christian Festivals with all pomp and circumstance and made much of other special occasions so as to enhance our students' lives. There were special dinners and dances and prize-giving days.

I enjoyed another stint in the maternity home, this time as a staff nurse, which included night duty as well. This was something new for me as I had never stayed up working all night before. Night time was a very special time and had a magic quality of its own. Sometimes new patients had to be admitted in the middle of the night, and babies had to be delivered while I assisted the midwife. This was always very exciting for me as I had far more responsibilities then than before during my student time, especially when two mothers gave birth at the same time and there were only two of us on duty. Then, I was left in charge until dilation was complete, before I could call the midwife, who was busy with the other birth. I was terrified that the baby's head would pop out before the midwife arrived, but all went well and according to plan at all times. Sometimes, a doctor had to be sent for, and I had to set out all the equipment, stay on hand, and almost 'wipe the doctors brow' during the difficult births. Sometimes ladies would come in by taxi during the night, saying that they had severe pains as they had eaten an unripe apple and they did not know what to do. They almost had the baby there and then on the front doorstep.

Then there were the tiny babies to be fed during the night, while their mothers had their important beauty sleep. First, I had to express their milk before they went to sleep so that I could feed their babies with their mother's milk. The time between 2.00 and 4.00 a.m. was the most difficult period to stay awake, as life seemed at its lowest ebb then. I prepared the midwife's dinner and completed all chores before struggling with sleep.

Often, this tedious time was broken by the unexpected visit of a police officer, on night patrol, who also found this a difficult time. I remember standing by the kitchen sink, washing up our dinner remains, when suddenly a strange face appeared at the window. This really scared me because the policeman used his torch to light his face from underneath, making him appear very ghost like and gruesome. Laughingly he knocked on the scullery door to be let in and then receive a welcome cup of tea. If the babies were fretful, he would let them play with his truncheon or help feed them. Sometimes, he would bring us fruit from the greengrocers when he had to look after the store while the owners were on holiday. Other times, he would share freshly baked goodies from the bakeries, where the bakers were also working during the night. Thus, time always passed quickly and often in amusing ways.

I found sleeping in the daytime easy and always settled down in my little bed very quickly. However, sometimes at the weekend, I would rise early and go to work at a nearby pub/restaurant, where they held wedding receptions or special celebratory dinners, and I would help with the washing up in order to earn a little extra pocket money to go towards my holidays. This would prove to be an escape from the norm rather than a job for me, as it was so different from my everyday activities. I thoroughly enjoyed the bustling activities at the restaurant and marvelled at the sumptuous food served up at these occasions. Any food or wine, even champagne, that was left over was for our consumption, and I felt like a guest at a feast, even if I did eat in the kitchen or scullery. I also enjoyed meeting people from every walk of life rather than just spend my time with unmarried mothers, students, or children, so I took every opportunity to work there, even if it meant to go without sleep at times.

Soon, my time at the maternity home passed, and I returned to the residential home, to resume my duties there. These were the same as before, but also included covering for the cook's day off, as well as the vice principal's whenever she was away. I had to instruct the maids as to what vegetables to prepare, what meats to get ready for cooking, as well as to see to the preparation of the day's puddings. Thus, I learnt not to be fazed by preparing and cooking breakfast, dinner, and high tea for seventy persons and laying out food for a late snack for the students. I also had to cater for baby and toddler food, children's and students' food, and lay special trays for Miss Gardner. Everything had to be done to a very high standard, and I had to follow certain rules.

As I did not know much about cooking or the preparation, thus I had a great deal to learn. I also had to put aside my shyness when dealing with the kitchen staff, who knew exactly what to do and would try me out, in my ignorance. I was a fast learner as necessity taught me well.

In the garden, Miss Gardner kept a pony as a pet for the children, and I had to feed it, which used to frighten me as I was not used to being with any animals.

The college also had a kindergarten, which was a proper nursery school for children three to five years old where children from the outside world and the nearby community could attend. This was run in exactly the same way as the state nursery schools. When the nursery teacher was absent, I had to run the school and take charge. I was always given a free hand to bring new ideas and methods into the college, after discussing them first with the principal, whom I respected greatly. She was a forward-thinking lady but never took to fools gladly. I enjoyed being somewhat of an entrepreneur and was pleased with the successes I managed to pull off.

I, too, had my regular days off when I could enjoy the freedom that I never had before to do as I wished. I could sleep in or stay in bed all day, go out into the town, or take the train to London and explore this fascinating city that I knew so little about. I would take the milk train at 5.00 a.m. to Paddington, London (this was the cheapest way to travel), and then follow a prepared plan of sightseeing, museum visits, and theatre visits. At last, I was once again able to enjoy the magic of the theatre. For the princely sum of one shilling and sixpence (seven pence) I could get a seat with the gods—the balcony. I would buy my ticket well in advance of the beginning of the performance and then queue to get the best seat high up in the gods. The theatre would put out little stools to sit on while waiting, and passing street entertainers would busk before us and keep us all amused.

When the timing was right, I would attend an early matinee at one theatre and then rush to another to get the early evening performance before returning home before midnight. I saw a great many plays and my favourite ones more than once. I often wished I had friends to go with on those occasions, but did not really mind being on my own. I was, however, scared when I had to walk back home from the station, as the last bus had long since departed. I always walked right in the middle of the road so that passing traffic could see me, and should any man be lurking in the shadows, ready to attack me, I would hear and see him coming so I could scream for help. Happily, nothing ever happened.

Back in Reading, I joined an amateur theatre club—the Progress Theatre, which enjoyed a good reputation. I attended all training classes and often auditioned to take part in performances of plays, but this was more difficult for me as my free time did not always coincide with rehearsal or performances. I often arrived late due to my work rota and was too embarrassed to go into the building, so I hung around outside, waiting for another latecomer, with whom I could sidle in. I made friends with another young girl, Iris Parker, who lived not far from my college, so we could walk home together and sometimes when my duties allowed have a cup of coffee in her flat during the day. When she got married she would enlighten me about sex, marital life, and what boys and girls get up to when in love. Never having had a boyfriend I found all that very interesting and somewhat scary, although of course I did know all about the birds and the bees.

I still continued playing with the Youth Orchestra whenever I could and sometimes even had time off in order to visit the cinema.

On some days off, I visited my cousin Resi and 'Aunty' Gizi, as well as making a trip to the hostel. Time always passed pleasantly enough. Life was good, and the years passed by contentedly.

I had lost touch with the Catholic Church and was too embarrassed to go and find a priest, as I did not know the procedure in England and had no idea of how to attend confession or mass in English. On the Continent, mass was always said in Latin, so everyone would get used to the language used and could follow the service. I missed a religious life and continued studying other religions by reading various books that discussed various beliefs. I also heard of a group led by a doctor who attended the children at the hostel and looked into joining the group. They studied the philosophy of a Russian called Ouspenski, which was an interesting and practical approach to life. He believed that we live in a very semi-conscious state and had to practice hard to reach a higher state of consciousness. We often just moved through the day automatically, wondering how we had arrived at a certain place or as to how many doorways we passed through without thinking. We were asked whether we ever experienced the real colour of the sky, the brightness of nature, and the beautiful smell of the flowers we passed. It made me think.

Yes, I did sometimes become aware of an intensity of light and colour when going about my daily tasks, but that always passed all too quickly. I was told that I would have to practice. Firstly, I had to count every doorway I passed and then think: did I really want to go through it or was I on autopilot? I was asked to note how often I wasted energy by doing something unnecessary. Only when we became more conscious of what we did in everyday life could we pass onto the next stage and progress up the ladder of complete consciousness, which would be the state nearest to God. I was fascinated by this approach and practised all I had to achieve each week. When work became too demanding and there was not enough time in the day for me to attend these meetings, I stopped going there but continued practicing awareness.

Flying in my dreams continued to be a regular pastime, and I visited many beautiful places in my dreams, often revisiting them at various times. By this stage, I could soar high in the sky and feel as free as a bird. Often, I would show off and complete little acrobatic exercises while flying and like an aeroplane at an air show dip and dive and do somersaults and generally enjoy the freedom of the sky.

I still visit some of these places in my dreams, although I have no idea whether they exist and where they are. I just loved flying and dreaming. It always left me with a feeling of contentment and real joy.

I was paid a regular salary of thirty shillings a week (one pound fifty) and opened my first bank account with Barclays Bank in Reading. Then, I could save for holidays or little extras that I wanted to buy. I did not need much. As I had little time to go out and as I had free board and lodging as well as a uniform to wear I managed to save quite easily.

My first present that I bought myself with my saved-up salary was a little travelling Phillip's radio. It looked like a small suitcase and could be played by using electricity or batteries. I was so proud of my purchase and kept it working for the next twenty years, or even longer.

The college used foreign students and unmarried mothers for domestic work. The foreign students could thus learn English, and the unmarried mothers, who had nowhere to go and often had been disowned by their families, could work and bide their time until their baby was due. They could then have it delivered in the maternity home and subsequently get help with adoption. Most of these were girls from good homes, and I made friends with many of them. My particular friend was a German girl from Berlin, named Christa, who came to England to learn English and was working at the Chilterns as a domestic. She was the same age as I and we could often get similar time off and spend it visiting places of interest or go on day's outings along the river Thames, visiting Oxford, Cambridge, or just go rambling. We received permission to coincide our yearly holiday and planned to go hitch hiking to Wales. We felt as free as birds and recited the German poem 'Wir sind jung und die Welt ist offen . . .' (We are young and the world is open . . .). We were lucky and had many good lifts from friendly strangers who would tell us what to see and where to stay. We saw and travelled all over Wales and marvelled at all nature's beauty. Too soon, the holiday finished, but we planned and were able to travel another time down to the West Country by hitchhiking in that part of the British Isles. We stayed friends for many years, even after she returned to Berlin to study and become a nursery teacher.

Life at the Chiltern Nursery Training College continued as before. I worked hard and enjoyed life.

I had lost touch with Slavka, my father's wife, after my father died. I often thought of my father and wished that I had really known him, especially as my interest in theatre life deepened. I would have loved to be able to discuss plays, productions, and players with him. Oh, why did I not write more to him and at least get to know him through his letters now that I was older?

News from Germany was not good. My parents had moved to Giessen, a university town in Hessen, where my stepfather obtained a post at a solicitors firm. He had also traced the whereabouts of his parents, who had been transported from Prague and had been sent to Germany to live just outside Frankfurt. Thus the family was reunited. My stepfather had complained for quite a few years of feeling tired, and it was thought that he suffered from jaundice and he was treated accordingly. Then everyone, including my mother, said he was just being lazy. Alas, the symptoms were not diagnosed correctly, and he died of leukaemia shortly afterwards. Then my mother was all alone again and on the breadline.

My little sister had contracted Perthes Disease—an inflammation of the head of the femur—with great pain in the hip and leg. She was hospitalized for a long time and put into traction. She then had to wear an iron leg brace for the next year or so, and being only eight years old needed much care and nursing. My mother found a much smaller flat in a house in Giessen and tried to find some part-time work to keep them both. As I had my bank account, I was able to arrange to send a monthly sum of three pounds over to Germany to help them a little. I also visited them during that unhappy time, bringing little goodies such as Nescafe and tea as well as biscuits and chocolates for them. I was very unhappy to see them both in such a plight and wished I could do more for them. Should I leave England and live in Germany, I wondered? That really would solve nothing at all as I was Anglicized by now and knew my way around British customs, whereas I had no idea of even how to use a telephone in Germany, and although I still spoke fluent German, I was not trained to do anything in that country. I was a foreigner there and thought of as being English. So I returned to the UK and sent what I could, both money and parcels.

My beautiful MOTHER

My handsome FATHER

My proud father

My parents 1932

My parents and I

Me in Prague outside our luxury flat

My daddy and I

My stage debut

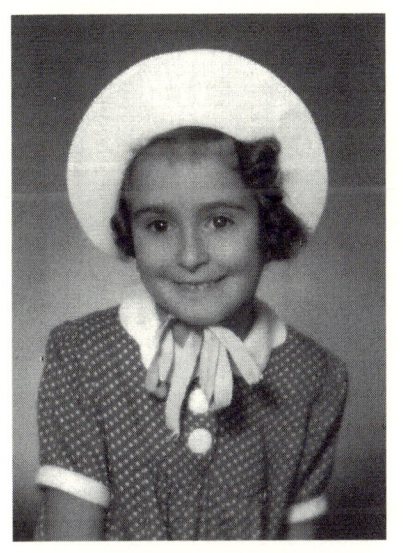

Just Little ME - 3 ½

Gee up horsey

My baby doll and I

Twin cousins and I

The THREE GRACES

Summer fun in Bavaria

My cousin Schorsch

My wonderful grandchidren

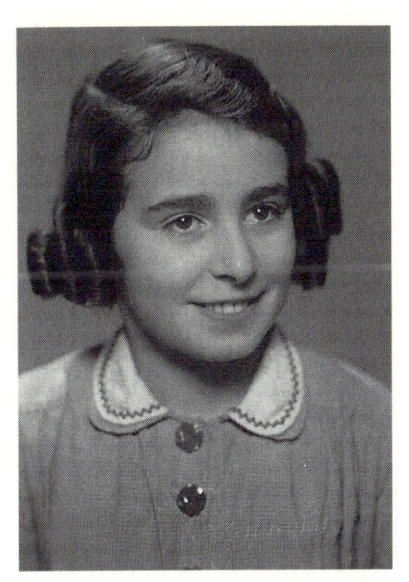

Passport photo for UK

My father, Slavka and I - post war Prague

Resi and Gizi in England

My mother and baby sister

My best friend and I

My sister's first school day

I am a proud Grammar School
Girl in England

Ski-ing in the Alps

Daisy the Nursery Nurse

Acting is in my blood

My trusty cyclemaster

My lovely BUBBLE CAR

Our Wedding Photograph

Honeymoon hitch-hiking

On Honeymoon in Olympia = Greece

Lucinda Black Velvet the Great Dane

Penelopy the Great Dane and Molly the English Setter

Our pony Lady - in the garden

My three little 'men'

My four children

My baby girl

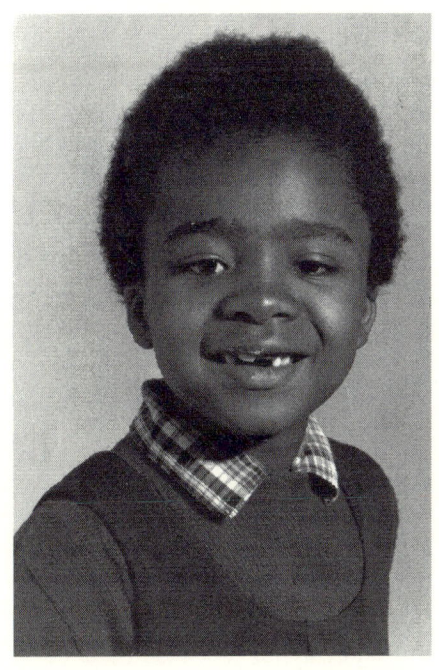

My lovely little foster daughter

My lovely family

Summer in Polzeath - Cornwall

Family is Growing up!

My mother and our pygmy goats in our garden

My mother and I visiting our eldest son at St Andrew's University

LA here I come

Visiting LA

The Headteacher

25 years wedding anniversary

Goodbye to our house 'The Bounty'

My wonderful grandchidren

Chapter 12

Back at the college, the principal sent for me. She explained that there were a couple of cottages on the grounds of the college, adjoining the residential home, and she had thought of the idea of turning them into a family group home with six children. She wanted me to run this little home with the help of a domestic (one of the unmarried mothers). I was delighted with this idea as it would be the first of its kind in England, and I could plan and execute everything. I went to look at the dilapidated building, ripped out everything, and painted all the rooms in bright colours. Next, I made colourful curtains and found furniture from around the college. Before long all was ready, and when inspected by the principal and approved of, I was able to move in with a baby, two toddlers, two nursery-aged children, and a school-aged child.

At last, I had my own little family to love and care for. I was mother and father to them and had sole charge. Food was sent over from the residential home kitchen, but I did all the laundry and cleaning with the help of my domestic. These kept changing as their birthing time drew nigh. To make this a more realistic home, I was able to take the oldest child to a nearby school and the nursery-aged children to a nursery within the college grounds. Babysitting became part of the job, but I did get a day off and even some evenings. I was so proud of my little family and begrudged every moment I was away from them. Time passed.

Christmas came, and my mother asked whether I could join them in Germany. I was absolutely delighted and excited to be invited once more to spend Christmas with my own family. When requesting permission to have a holiday, I was reminded that I was mother to six children, and it would not be kind to them to leave them at this time. Oh, I could understand all the reasoning and agree with it, but I myself was still a teenager who badly wanted her mother. Alas, everything had to be postponed. I was told that I could invite my mother and sister to come and spend a holiday with me in the summer. To hide my disappointment, I planned ahead for the summer.

I continued with my little family group and was happy. Once I remarked to the principal that it was a shame I could not breast feed my baby, and she took me quite serious and said that if I really wanted to, I should try and milk would come. What a bizarre idea. I never tried this idea of hers.

Summer came around with the usual regularity, and my mother really did arrive with my sister to stay with me. Proudly, I showed her around and took them both to London sightseeing. I also took them to the cinema to see some Rodger and Hammerstein musicals, which we loved and cried all the way through. What a pair of sillies we were. On one of my days off, I took them both on a coach trip to the seaside at Hayling Island. It was a very overcast day, but warm, so we enjoyed swimming and lying on the beach. On our return home we felt our faces burning and by the next day suffered with real sunburn. I was hauled before the principal and told off for being so irresponsible so as to get us burned. How was I to know that the sunlight would filter very strongly through the cloud layer, thus magnifying the rays? I had no experience of life by the sea and thought it unfair to be made to feel guilty. The rest of my mother's holiday passed without a mishap, and soon we had to be parted yet again.

Throughout this time, life at the hostel continued in the same way with children coming and going. I saw them only seldom. Sadly, I lost touch during this time with my best school friends who had gone onto university while I was left behind.

Change, too, affected Resi and Gizi. I saw both of them occasionally and always had to make special appointments before being able to visit.

This took all the pleasure of an impromptu visit for me, and hence visits became infrequent. Both ladies continued their work, when suddenly Gizi announced that she was leaving the UK to go and marry her cousin and live in Belgium. Resi, too, had been courting a gentleman named Frank. Slowly, a friendship developed between the two of them.

Before long, the two of them bought a bungalow in Wokingham and moved in together, marrying as soon as Frank could obtain a divorce. Frank was a lovely, kind, and gentle man who always had a kind word for me. I visited them in their home for many years to come but relationships stayed lukewarm and were more of a family tie than a feeling of love. Sadly, Resi had no one but me left from her big Bendiner family, and I was the only link to her past.

When I performed in plays or orchestral concerts (now having joined the Reading Symphony Orchestra an amateur society) neither she or Hilde and Sophie came to applaud me, and I so much wanted to be thought of as good and talented by people close to me. Everyone was always very quick to criticize but never praised me.

My twenty-first birthday was drawing near, and to my great surprise, Miss Halliday, the principal, decided to throw a dinner and dance to celebrate this special occasion. I bought an evening dress and felt very sophisticated and grown-up but nervous, as I had never been to a dance and had not learnt how to dance. But this was my special day, and everyone went out of their way to make it a happy occasion with laughter, music, dancing, and fine food—no men! Neither Resi nor Hilde and Sophie attended, but that was not surprising. My mother sent me a special parcel and my friends, the Lattos, who I continued to visit, also sent me gifts. I felt very special and very grateful to Miss Halliday for this auspicious occasion. Never had anyone taken so much trouble or thought about me or any of my birthdays.

Work, holidays, and special occasions punctuated my life at that time, but I became restless and felt I wanted to achieve greater things in life than running a little family group. My thoughts took fanciful flights, looking at various options. A theatrical career was uppermost in my mind as I so loved the world of make belief. As my salary had increased over the time,

I managed to save a little money and bought myself a cyclemaster—a motorised bicycle. With that I rode to London every week, and four hours later, with a sore bottom, visited a place for speech and drama in order to prepare some speeches so that I could audition at the Old Vic Theatre. This bastion of English theatrical heritage beckoned me and I was determined to try and set foot inside this theatre where I had seen so many wonderful productions. Proudly, I stood on the stage and performed Lady Macbeth's letter speech, followed by a speech from *Twelfth Night*. There was no rapturous applause, but a voice out of the darkness of the auditorium asked me what my accent was, as I seemed to have a Welsh or South African lilt—only true Queen's English could be spoken on that hallowed stage. No accents were allowed. Hence, I received the answer 'Do not call us; we will call you'.

Next I tried to audition for Royal Academy of Dramatic Art so that I could receive a good training. I knew nothing of grants or help available through the educational services, so I informed them at my interview that I could only come if they offered me one of their few free places. Alack and alas—no glamorous and glitzy life for me; neither fame nor fortune was to beckon me.

Well Daisy, dear, be sensible and look towards a more practical vocation. Did you not always want to become a doctor? Well you were stopped schooling and did not have the higher exam results needed for a university place. So how about becoming a nurse and then marrying a doctor? Not a bad idea!

I therefore applied to the Radcliffe Hospital in Oxford for admission and this time was successful in my quest. I was offered a place but thinking it through, I found that I did not want to go back to being a skivvie, cleaning bedpans, and generally being a dogsbody after I had enjoyed all that responsibility at the college. Anyway, who could say that I would meet a doctor who would want to marry me? So that, too, became a no—no.

Would I consider becoming a fully qualified midwife instead? No—it was all about breasts and bums, and I had seen enough of those by now.

Next, I tried and was accepted for training as a physiotherapist at Guy's Hospital, London. I was very excited as I entered the corridors of the hospital and then was shown round. When I was shown the electrical instruments and appliances that have to be utilized when treating patients, after having first experienced them ourselves, I just panicked. I was afraid of electricity and could not abide electrical shocks or electrical stimulation of any kind. How was I to survive? Very ashamed of myself that I had not checked out all the facts, I left the hospital, never to return there again. Another failure.

I decided to leave my future well alone for the time being and continue enjoying my work at the Chiltern Training College and stayed there for seven more years.

Chapter 13

I HAD MANY INTERESTING HOLIDAYS while I worked at the college. During one of them, I decided to hitchhike by myself up to Scotland in order to see the country and to attend the Edinburgh Festival. I packed a rucksack and set off on the A1, heading north. There were no motorway at that time, so all major roads were the A roads. At first, all went well and I was lucky in meeting nice people, who were both helpful and informative. Then when there seemed to be a lull in the traffic, I decided to hail a lorry, which seemed to be going my way. The driver was jovial and friendly—too friendly, as I found out a little later.

We were travelling steadily along the A1, when his hands started to wander along my knees and up my skirt. I brushed his hand off and said I was not that kind of girl, but he was most persistent, saying he had a comfy cabin behind the driver's seat and we could have some fun. By this time, I had become very panicky, and said I would jump from the lorry and started to try and open the door. Reluctantly, the driver pulled in to the side of the road and became very abusive, at which I opened the door, grabbed hold of my luggage, jumped out, and disappeared behind a nearby hedge. It was dark by then, and I could not see where I was going or what awaited me behind the hedge.

Then, I just ran. I crouched low in the field and hardly dared to breathe until I heard the lorry drive off. I dared not move all night long, and as it was dark and misty I had no idea where I was. I imagined all sorts of horrors in the field with me, I saw outlines of cows, which I was sure were bulls and therefore did not move from my crouching position. At last, day dawned, and I could see cows grazing some way away from where I had squatted all night. I crawled out of the field and walked along the road, debating with myself as what to do next. I decided that one bad experience should not cloud my judgement, so continued my hitchhiking to the North. For the rest of my journey, I had nothing but good experiences with interesting people.

I learnt all about work in Yorkshire, open-cast coal mining, and pottery and was told interesting titbits of historical events in all the regions that I passed through. At night, I stayed in youth hostels and enjoyed the company of other travellers. Before long, I reached the majestic city of Edinburgh and was quite bowled over by the architectural beauty of all the buildings and the way in which the castle dominated the city. The Scottish city reminded me of my beloved Prague both in architecture and atmosphere. The youth hostel was full, but I found lodgings in an inexpensive bed and breakfast place. There I met other hopefuls who wanted to see the varied events of the Edinburgh Festival. Together, we all set forth to book what tickets were available and then were told how to get in to some of the fully booked venues on the day or how to attend the final dress rehearsals. The festival was not due to start for another week, so I decided to hitch around Scotland to see some of the beauty spots.

I visited Loch Lomond and made my way up to the 'Weeping Glen' where so many brave Scots were killed during their battles. To make Glencoe even more mysterious, a mist had descended and a fine rain covered everything. My imagination took flight and made me very sad when thinking of all that useless slaughter.

Next, I went to Ben Nevis but only managed a little walk up the majestic slopes, as a mist covered the summit and time was passing so quickly and dusk began to fall. The Isle of Skye proved to be very wet and the journey in 'speed bonny boat' was choppy and cold. I landed, had a cup of tea, and returned to the mainland, to continue to John O'Groats, via Inverness, and pay my respects to Nessie, the Loch Ness Monster. She was 'not at home' so I had to imagine everything as I gazed at the vast lake,

After John O'Groats, I made my way to Balmoral, to admire the castle, pay my respects in Crathie Church, and then enjoy the beautiful, lush scenery of the countryside. All the pine forests reminded me of Bavaria, and I felt very happy to spend time there but was disappointed not to be invited to have tea with the Queen.

I had to get back to Edinburgh for the start of the Festival, so I continued my journey via the famous Devil's Elbow to Sterling. A quick look at the castle there and off for the final lap to the Scottish capital. It was a wonderful trip, and I revelled in the beautiful scenery, loved the colourful heather, and was fascinated by the long-haired Highland cattle, which looked so regal as they grazed in their fields.

Edinburgh was stunning, and I enjoyed walking along Princes' Street.

I had booked my place at the B&B before I had left, so there was no accommodation problem for me. I went to see Hamlet three times as I loved Richard Burton's Hamlet and Clair Bloom's Ophelia. I also attended many other plays and concerts, often as dress rehearsals. Wonderful!

The time flew past very quickly, but as I had seen a great deal I did not mind too much. Somewhere along the way, a young man attached himself to me and wanted to join me attending various venues. I did not care for him, and anyway distrusted men, thinking they were only after one thing. I tried hard to evade him, and one day lost him by joining a nearby crowd.

Suddenly, I found myself standing next to Richard Burton and Claire Bloom, but they took no notice of me. Richard Burton did not wish to pursue me, as the young man had done—even though according to my grandmother I looked like Elizabeth Taylor—for that would have been quite a different thing altogether.

My time had come to an end and I took the train back to Reading to start work again.

Soon after my arrival back at the college, I received a little bouquet of orchids from the spotty young man who would not leave me in peace in

Edinburgh. I do not know how he got my address, and as I never answered his note, he never wrote again.

Another chapter in my life had passed, and I soon settled down to work again.

Chapter 14

My next holiday was a skiing trip to Austria. I used to ski as a child in Bavaria and longed for the snow and the winter wonderland that appeared every year as if by magic. I could hardly wait to see everything covered with white 'icing sugar' and see icicles decorating the gutters as they hung from the rooftops and sparkled in the winter sunshine.

I researched various travel companies and booked in with Inghams to ski in Alpbach, Austria. The package included ski hire, lift passes, and all-day ski school. The train left from Victoria, and we travelled overnight. I slept on the luggage rack, which proved to be quite comfortable. Eventually, we arrived in Alpbach, and it seemed to me that we just stepped right into a fairy-story book. The village was quaint, with lovely Austrian, wooden houses, decorated with wood carvings and painted in bright colours. The bedrooms were cosy and warm, and I at last had my beloved feather bed to snuggle under. The food reminded me of Bavaria and my grandmother's cooking—delicious. I was in Heaven.

Up bright and early I joined the ski school on the nursery slopes, having been fitted up with all the gear. I learnt skiing from the very beginning and was soon flying down the slopes. I felt so at home in Austria and was able to speak German and even use my Bavarian dialect. I seemed to know all the German songs, sung at that time. I do not know where from. They must have been ingrained into my brain when I was a baby and heard my father's operettas, or I had learnt some of the many folk songs when at the German school or even the Hitler Youth. After a week's holiday I was well and truly hooked and vowed to come skiing every winter. For a wild moment I thought of handing in my notice at the Chiltern and become a ski rep for Inghams and help teaching skiing on the nursery ski slopes. That, however, was not a sound idea at all, even if very tempting.

More short-break holidays to Germany followed, and I stayed at the various flats my mother was living in at the time. I always felt gauche and frumpy when with her as I could not live up to her ideal of a young woman. One autumn, whilst I was visiting, we drove down to Bavaria to see my grandmother and aunts, who I had missed so much. I was so excited to be able to see Pegnitz once again and meet my aunts after all this time. I got a fabulous welcome, and we talked and talked until deep into the night. I told them all about my life in England, my joys, and my fears. My cousin Schorsch, appeared as if by magic, having cycled thirty miles, and we became once more inseparable. We had such fun, trying to relive memories of the past.

My grandmother was appalled that at twenty-one years old I was not yet married and had no beaux. She began immediately to introduce me to various bachelors, praising their possibilities. They were usually farm labourers or lorry drivers with whom I had nothing in common and did not wish to be seen dead with. My grandmother, on the other hand, thought any man is better than none and I should be so lucky if one of them fancied me. She even brought a very distant cousin of fifty years or more to be introduced to. He had part shares of our cinema, and she thought old or not, I would be well off living with him. Luckily, nothing became of all these introductions. However, my cousin Christa's fiancé paid me more attention than he should have and actually invited me to travel with him in his lorry when he went to fetch fresh vegetables from Munich, as I had never been to this fair city. He was a greengrocer and had to replenish his stores every week, but once that was done, he could show me round Munich. Oh dear me, suddenly I was the wicked temptress who would seduce the young men of the village and was packed off to travel back with my mother. I was so sad to leave my cousin but we were told that we must not be so fond of each other as we were blood relatives and any relationship between us would be impossible. Nothing was further from our mind—we just loved each other in the biblical sense of brother and sister. There were more sad goodbyes and an eminent return to the British Isles.

Having seen many films in our cinema during my short stay in Pegnitz, I sat in the train and dreamt of Zorro coming to rescue me and sweep me off my feet. Dream on, my girl.

I began daydreaming of being loved and being wanted by someone special. I started having imaginary friends with whom I could talk and who would console me when I was sad and lonely. They were good company and would never scold or put me down.

Would I ever have a boyfriend, I wondered. As I seemed to mistrust the male sex and thought they were only after sex, as Hilde and Sophie had told me, I thought it very unlikely that I should find someone. I did, however, want children and a whole family of my own instead of always looking after other people's children. I even toyed with the idea of asking Dr Latto if he would be interested in impregnating me, as at the time there were no sperm banks. How ridiculously was that! Still I was still young, and my biological clock was far from ticking time away. I decided to travel and enjoy myself.

Once I was twenty-one-years-old, I could apply for my British citizenship, so I enquired about the procedure and collected all relevant papers. Once these were completed, I sent them off and awaited the great day when I would no longer be stateless, a foreigner, or an alien. In Britain, everyone looked at me as if I were different—one would think I had come from outer space. There were very few people from Europe, Africa, or India to be seen in Britain in those years. These groups immigrated in larger numbers at a later date. I was German, Jewish, Catholic, and Czech, and I had to take people's abuse for not being British. Once naturalised, I could belong to a great country and be proud to be its citizen.

The day approached when I would have to swear my oath of allegiance. I was told to look for a commissioner of oaths and make an appointment for the final stage of becoming British. For the stately sum of twenty pounds, I was invited to attend the commissioner's offices. Alack and alas, there were no fanfares, no roll on the drums, and no 'gilded' official to welcome me. I had dressed in new clothes and had brushed and polished myself to look like a new pin. I entered the seedy office, which was dark and drab. The commissioner of oaths pushed a piece of paper in front of me, put a Bible into my hand, and asked me to read what was written. Before I knew what was happening I found myself outside his doors once again.

I was so disappointed. At the least I had wanted to sing 'I vow to thee my country, all earthly things above . . .' and to swear allegiance to this Sceptred Island, set in a jewelled sea. I had built myself up for this auspicious moment when I would be accepted by the British people and once again belong somewhere. What could I say or do? I went home, and the joy of the moment had been taken from me—no bright lights, no party, and no one to rejoice with. I was British now but still all alone. My one comfort was that now I could get a British passport and travel freely without having all those problems of being stateless person and needing countless visas.

I could go skiing again! That surely was something to look forward to.

As before, *tempus fugit,* and another year had passed. It was time to make a change in my life, but how? While I was debating with myself as to what path to follow, I thought it would be fun to work as a *Huetten picke*—a chalet girl in Norway. I could ski there as well as meet many more people not connected with childcare. I found a vacancy but could not get the necessary work permits. It was another dead end.

Well, if I could not become a paediatrician, but wanted to continue working with children, who gave me so much pleasure, then I should become a teacher. I fully explored this idea, and I asked all sorts of people for advice. I also found out that I could get a scholarship or grant and have my studies paid for by the Borough of Reading. I researched information about a suitable training college and found that Trent Park Teachers' Training College, part of the University of London, would be the ideal place as it specialized in drama and also catered for mature students like me who had worked beforehand.

I went to see my old head teacher at Kendrick Grammar School, who was delighted that I would study at last and she said again how sorry she was when my guardian did not let me stay on and get a university place in order to become a doctor. She steered my way to the right department at the education office where I could get grants so that I could apply to the college of my choice. To my great joy I was accepted, attended interviews and induction days, and was shown around the college. I was so taken with the beautiful country house built by Sir Philip Sassoon, which was set in vast grounds with magnificent gardens, a lake, and adjacent farmlands. I felt like a queen and thought myself to be so privileged to be able to live there for a while that I opted for the full two-year course, which pleased the principal.

I still had to wait nine months before I could start my course, so I handed in my notice at the college where I had worked for seven years in order to gain some work experience outside the world of education.

I found a post as reference clerk at Huntley and Palmers, the biscuit factory in Reading, and started to work in their offices. I made new friends and settled quickly into office work, learning all the new skills needed for a secretarial post. I really enjoyed my new job and the challenges it brought. I thrived when I had to deal with all the customers' queries and solve their problems.

I also joined their drama club and performed in a few plays while working there.

I moved into a one-room bed-sitter, for the price of one pound ten a week. I saved hard and ate only the least expensive food. One of the perks of working at Huntley and Palmers was that we could get a box of broken biscuits for just a few pence. This supplemented my food bill. I loved my new life and made the most of it, knowing that once the new academic year started I would go to university.

I joined the Reading Operatic Society and took part in a couple of shows, making a memorable impression on the critics. I also met a couple of interesting guys and joined them when they produced their own musical about *Pride and Prejudice* that they had just written. I really liked the older man, Geoffrey, and he occasionally came to see me in my little flat, so I could help him with his lines. He was at the time in a Shakespeare play, *King Lear*, and found it useful to have someone helping him learning all those very long speeches. I would also go to his house and clean the place. I just wanted to be needed. He explained to me that he was in a homosexual relationship, and his friend was jealous of our friendship. We could not continue seeing each other. I was sad as I wanted to be needed and feel protected, and I thought this to be just an excuse and he did not really like me. I knew nothing about homosexual relationships and thus could not understand the petty jealousies. I was learning the hard way.

During the rehearsals of *Oklahoma* at the operatic society I became aware that the musical director took a special interest in me. This was balm for my wounded soul. We became friends, and when it turned out that he too had trained at Trent Park Training College, we saw each other often.

He introduced me to his family, where I was a welcome guest. It was great to feel cherished by someone. On opening day at Trent Park, he took me up to London in his car and showed me all around the college. On the way home, we had dinner out and then stopped in a lonely lay by in the country, where he made sexual advances to me, kissing and cuddling. I had never been kissed before as I had never had a boyfriend in my life and was in seventh heaven. He asked me to come on a week's holiday before I started college, and I agreed to go camping with him, but explained that only as a sister, as I wanted to keep myself for the right man when the time came. Old fashioned or not, that was what I wanted. He agreed.

We had a lovely holiday and during that week he proposed to me, with diamond ring that he just happened to have after a previous engagement had failed. I was delighted and accepted. Now, I would no longer be lonely but would belong to someone who would take care of me. On the last night of our holiday, while sleeping in our little tent in a forest, I succumbed to his caresses and lost my virginity in that silent, beautiful wood, with nothing but the full moon, stars, and woodland spirits watching over me and bear witness to me becoming a full-blown woman.

At last, the day drew nigh, and I packed up my little flat and the furniture that was given to me by the hostel some time ago, I stored it with the Latto family. I had a letter that I was going to live in digs with a family in East Barnet, not far from the college, so Paul, my fiancé, drove my belongings up to London, and I followed on my newly bought Lambretta scooter. The cyclemaster bike had become too slow, and I had fallen in love with the sleek, fast motor scooter. Life was exciting.

I now was a proper student at a real university—the University of London—and I lapped up the academic life. I belonged and did not feel a foreigner. I was just another student. I found studying easy and did not spend over much time with my books. Instead, I joined all the societies and learnt painting, drama, and nature study. We would spend endless hours walking around the beautifully laid out parkland or just sit by the lake philosophising. I became a close friend of a lady, who like me was a mature student. Her name was Barbara Lippitt, and as she lived in her own house nearby, I often went home with her and enjoyed some home comforts. I also became a very close friend with a man named Gordon Vallins from Eastbourne who was on the drama course with me, and we would often disappear for the afternoon and evening in order to go to the West End of London and see various plays. As part of our course we needed to see many shows, write reviews, and be able to discuss many current plays being performed in London. We had great fun together, laughing and talking all day long. One evening, while walking through Soho, he got mugged for no reason at all but luckily was not hurt apart from a few bruises and a damaged ego.

'Daisy, if you have to get hurt or get run over, be sure to choose a Rolls Royce and do things in good style. Nothing but the best for you my girl,' he would jest.

Oh, we had many good times together, and I was even invited to visit his home in Eastbourne and meet his parents. He really was an excellent friend.

My flying dreams continued and became more adventurous, and I often visited many exciting places.

During the day, when I felt lonely and longed for loving arms to protect and comfort me, I resorted once again to daydreaming and 'talked' to my imaginary friend, who had been with me for so many years.

Lectures were always interesting, and we had very good and knowledgeable lecturers. Our psychology lecturer was a lady who looked rather like Margaret Rutherford.

She had been an ardent skier and was a member of the Ski Club of Great Britain and on hearing that I too enjoyed that sport, nominated me for membership to the Club.

Mr Millar, our science and religious instruction lecturer was a fascinating character. He would take us on nature walks around the park and point out all the famous trees—the Judas tree, the Tulip tree, and many others—planted in glorious array around the parkland. Nothing was left to chance and everything was planted to the best advantage possibly. The science lectures consisted of practical and scientific experiments for the children we would eventually teach. They were interesting and full of fun.

Far more interesting however, were the religious studies lectures. Mr Millar would talk about various chapters from the Bible and explain how they could have happened: for instance, the falling of the walls of Jericho. They did not have deep foundations, and when the approaching army was told to march round and round the city walls, the vibrations set up would eventually cause the walls to crumble and then give way completely to the joy of the invaders and horror of the inhabitants.

The parting of the waters of the Red Sea he explained away as being a natural process at certain times due to draught, dams, and flooding. There were many stories that he told us which seemed to make sense, without taking away any religious implications.

Later, I discovered *King Jesus,* a book written by Robert Graves, which absolutely fascinated me. It also discussed some of the Bible miracles, such as the healing of the blind. It was a fact that flies could lay eggs in the eyes of people and set up infections that rendered them blind. Jesus sent these people down to the water's edge of the river Jordan, which to this day has very therapeutic mud and now even has pharmaceutical factories there. Jesus would put on a thick layer of this mud on the blind people's eyes and ask them to leave it on for a week, and then wash it all off. The medical properties of the mud disinfected the eyes, the water cleansed the face, and with the infection gone, the blind could see again.

The book also paid tribute to the knowledge of epileptic fits, sleeping sickness, and other diseases that made sick people fall into a death-like trance. When this passed, the 'dead' could be woken, and life could continue as before. There are many other such examples in Robert Graves's book, and I was avid reader and studied them all.

The two years spend at Trent Park was divided between lectures and practical work at school placements. I enjoyed being with the children aged between seven and eleven in different types of schools. I was given a timetable to follow and told which lessons I had to prepare for. Then I had full charge of the class and was left on my own with them. Lecturers and teachers would look in and observe my lessons and then discuss my teaching progress. I really enjoyed these placements and could not wait to have a real job and a class of my own.

Lectures of psychology, philosophy, history, art, drama, music, and many others connected to teaching, continued throughout the two years. Often, I would skip lectures, particularly PE and invent numerous monthly women's troubles and take myself off to the West End of London to see plays, films, or visit art galleries. I also joined the college orchestra and revived my skills on the cello.

Time passed much too quickly.

During this time, I lived with the Willis family in East Barnet. They were an elderly couple and staunch Methodists. I must have been quite an eye opener at times for them. They were very kind and supportive in every way. Mr Willis would always want to help me with practical preparations for my teaching practice, and Mrs Willis would listen to my stories about college. They also welcomed Paul, my fiancé, whenever he wanted to come and visit. Paul and I would discuss teaching, his music, and we would plan for the future. I began to be less keen on an immediate future with him, as he procrastinated with most things and was quite happy to continue living at home with his mother and sisters and where Paul wanted me to live with him.

Gordon Vallins would also come and visit the house, and both the Willises thought him to be a very nice, and eligible young man. Sometimes, we would cuddle in the front parlour and I would get all sorts of strange feelings of arousal, but we never overstepped the mark and laughed things off.

As always, I tried to diet, as the unkind words from Hilde and Sophie about being fat rang in my ears at all times. Thus, I tried avoiding stodgy puddings provided by Mrs Willis at the evening meal. She was not a very good cook and the food was watery and tasteless, but I had been brought up to eat everything on my plate. I asked her if I could finish my meals with soup instead of puddings, and though she found this most odd, she agreed to my request. She probably though it was just another heathen, Continental custom of mine.

During the university holidays I had to leave my lodgings, and as I had nowhere to go and in any case needed to earn some money, I signed up at the Nursery Nurses Bureau and was sent to different families as a nanny. They were all well-to-do people, and I relished living in style in their luxury apartments or houses in London. I always had full charge of the children and enjoyed the responsibility. I had to wear my nurse's uniform and was referred to as nanny.

One family lived near the BBC in Portland Place in a very luxurious flat. The parents always went away on holiday and left me with their two children. I had to shop, cook, and generally care for the children. The porter in his smart uniform, who guarded the front doors, always had a friendly word for me and advised me where I should go shopping and which park was nearby. We had fun and thank God no mishaps. The parents were very happy with me and asked me back during several holidays, and I was well paid for my troubles.

Another family just had a new baby, and the mother did not know how to care for it, so I, once more, had full command of the nursery wing and could run things as I thought best. I had my uses. They gave me such glowing references that I could hardly believe they wrote about me.

A family, living in their grand luxury flat in Highgate, adopted me as their nanny for their three children, whenever they needed me. I also used to babysit for them during term time. Sometimes, I was left alone with them while the parents went away on business or on holiday, and other times, I was invited to go along with them to Switzerland or Italy and look after the children all day long as well as in the evening. Everything was paid for, and I received a good salary. Mind you, they wanted 'a pound of flesh' for their generosity.

More notches to add to my belt of life's experiences.

I was always welcomed back home into the Willis household after each holiday and resumed my studies with gusto. Pub visits and parties were also part of student life, but I was always sad that no-one found me sexually attractive and wanted to make advances to me or even slip his hand under my jumper to undo my bra. Why not? What was wrong with me? Well, Gordon liked me as did Trevor and others in my Primary School Group, even if it was not as a sex goddess. Anyway, I was engaged to Paul! But it would have been good to be able to be a siren at least once.

Sometimes after parties, when there were no buses, I would give friends a lift home on my Lambretta, and at other times I would offer lifts to students on their way to college when they had to walk the long, winding lane that led up to the mansion. One night after a party, I gave two of my friends a lift and was stopped by a policeman as there were three of us on the small motor scooter. He asked how many this vehicle was built for, and I replied that it took three comfortably but if he wanted to jump on we could always try if it would take four! Trying to look stern, he asked me for my registration number and I had to get off the bike to have a look. When asked to produce my driving licence and registration papers, I said they were at home but declined to be accompanied by him to my lodgings as Mr and Mrs Willis would indeed be shocked to find an officer of the constabulary at their door. With promises not to repeat this feat, to drive carefully, and to be a responsible road user, I departed smiling, and the officer could hardly contain his mirth. Oh, those were good times!

Soon, my final term approached, and I had exams as well as a final teaching practice. I had planned a topic on houses with the eight-year-olds and thought it more stimulating to actually build some early dwellings in the school field. That exercise was most successful. We had grown cress in the classroom, and I decided to combine science and cookery by baking some brown bread. As this was still a time when children received free school milk, I collected the cream off all the children's milk and then put this into jars. The children had to shake these until the cream formed into butter and that could be spread onto the freshly baked bread. We all enjoyed these lessons, as did the examiner, and I passed with distinction.

Studies finished, we all said a fond farewell and promised to meet again in ten years' time to see how we got on.

I was very excited to get my first teaching placement in London in the Borough of Haringey in a junior school on Rhodes Avenue. I would have forty eight year olds to teach and be in sole charge of. I could hardly wait for the new school year to start.

But first I had to find somewhere to live and was lucky enough to find a really nice flat nearby, which occupied the entire top floor of a terraced house in Middelton Road in Bounds Green. The owner let me have it at a very good rent, and I was allowed to decorate the flat as I wanted. Armed with various colours and paint brushes, but very little knowledge, I learnt all about house painting as I went along and kind shopkeepers gave me plenty of advice.

I set about making the flat my home. It was fully but sparsely furnished, so I bought pictures, ornaments, and kitchen utensils and made new curtains and cushions to make it homely, comfortable, and welcoming.

I now was ready to embark on another chapter in my life, full of dreams and hopes for a successful future.

Chapter 15

The long-awaited day dawned when I would start my real teaching career. I had bought new clothes, had a haircut, and generally smartened myself to look like a respectable teacher. Would I be liked? Would I be accepted as one of the team or be looked upon as a foreigner? I was excited and full of hope that now at last I would fit in with everyone else. My heart was in my mouth when I first set foot in the school for the beginning of term staff meeting. I was shown around the place and led to my classroom that was to be my home for the next year. The staff meeting was interesting and informative, and I met all my colleagues but forgot their names as soon as the meeting was over. How would I be able to remember forty children's names that were in my class if I could not remember a handful of teachers' names? Still, if the others could, so could I.

The next day, school started in earnest. I was the second-year teacher in the junior school, with a bright and lively class of forty-eight eight-year-olds. The children having been in the school for a year were able to help me find my way around, and we all had a very successful and interesting day. I was in my element and loved every minute of it. The school's intake was from a very good area with parents from a wide background. The children therefore were bright and enjoyed a good level of intelligence and varied background experiences.

Teaching was a real joy to me, and I made everything as interesting as I could. The Head and parents were well satisfied with the standard of work produced.

Discipline was good, and I was strict as well as a good friend. Once, when some children were chatting and causing a disruption, I decided to keep the ringleader in after school. Alas, I had mistakenly kept in the wrong girl, and that not being enough, I left the room to complete some task and then forgot all about her and went home. The cleaner found her and sent her home. Her parents were very understanding when I told them of my plight and said their daughter had not said anything to them and, as no harm had been done, to forget the whole episode. I was very grateful to the parents and apologized to the girl in question. I never forgot this particular incident.

I had learnt a good lesson, and after I apologized to the girl, discussed everything with the class, as a lesson in life.

I took on various after-school clubs and enjoyed being with the children of various ages.

My flat was my comfortable home, and Paul often came to visit me, but I was so disappointed with his lack of drive and lack of initiative. His visits became boring and a great drag.

I chose to babysit and invited my charges from Highgate to stay with me. We had good and exciting times together, so one day when Paul joined us, I returned his engagement ring to him and wished him well. I thought we could continue just being friends, but I never saw him again. I suppose the engagement ring was used again, the next time he proposed to someone. Well, I wished him good luck as he was a nice and decent person, and I hoped that someone else would find him interesting and be a good wife to him. I certainly could not fulfil that role.

Friends of mine who were still at Trent Park had run into trouble. Audrey had become pregnant and was not married. She and her partner Colin needed somewhere to stay, as they could no longer stay in college rooms. Audrey was actually thrown out of the college by the principal for carrying an illegitimate child, while Colin could stay on and finish his training. How unfair was that! My flat seemed big, and I did not really need all those rooms, so I let them have my big sitting room and would share the kitchen with them, while I took the single room. This arrangement worked well, but sadly Audrey found out that the baby in her womb had died at eight months and she had to carry the dead infant until she started labour in the normal way. I could think of nothing worse that could happen to an expectant mother. Sometimes life really did not seem to be very fair. We all tried our best to cheer her up and the couple continued living with me as before.

Although I was happy with my new life, I felt a lack of companionship and still searched for love. I therefore joined a certain introduction agency in Bond Street that I had read about. They screened their clients and had a very good clientele. I was introduced to a gentleman and, when he telephoned me, decided to meet him outside Bounds Green tube station. He seemed very pleasant, and we set off in his car to take afternoon tea outside Potter's Bar. The earth did not move for either of us, so we just parted after a polite thank you for the afternoon.

My mother, in the meantime, had 'landed on her feet by becoming a personal secretary to a blind judge. She became his eyes and ears and during the day and generally was at his beck and call. His wife had helped out before that but wanted to follow her own career. They all became firm friends and even went skiing together during their holiday. My mother felt fulfilled with her new job and was very happy. My sister had grown into a young lady and, although never losing her slight limp, managed to attend ballroom dancing lessons and join in dances attired like a beautiful princess. She excelled in school and later university, where she too trained as a teacher. Of course through my mother's eyes, everything was so much better in Germany than in England and my sister's career was far more impressive than mine could ever be. I remained the Cinderella.

School and teaching became everything in my life and I worked hard. Having saved up some money, I exchanged my Lambretta for a bubble car. I had been told that I could drive the bubble car with my motorcycle licence as long as the reverse was shut off. I found a lovely little car and with the help of Mr Willis and some washers, stopped the reverse gear being used. Next, I had to learn to drive this little car. Again Mr Willis was helpful. I was thrilled and delighted to be a car driver. Now, I could drive everywhere in the warm and the dry during bad weather.

I took visitors and friends around London in my little car. One day, when I had four passengers instead of two, I drove right through the middle of London to show them the Houses of Parliament and Big Ben. Right in front of the clock tower I stalled and could not get the car moving again. A frustrated policeman waved me on but I held my breath hoping he would not notice that I had too many passengers. I apologized that I stalled and begged him to push my car to the side. He smiled and helped me out and never mentioned my crowded car.

I managed to get through many scrapes in my little bubble car that I loved dearly.

Still lonely, and finding no luck with an introduction agency, I guessed that this was no way for me to meet a future partner, although to me it had seemed a sensible way. I therefore decided to throw myself into evening activities. I found no drama club or orchestra at that time, so I decided to take up evening class teaching instead. I applied to the Wood Green Adult Education College and was interviewed by the principal, Mr Mac. He took a liking to me and put me forward to teach German as soon as a vacancy arose. I did worry about that as I had never learnt German grammar and wondered how I would get on. I supposed I could stay one chapter ahead of my pupils and at other times work things out backwards from the spoken German, in which I was fluent.

I was still in the first few weeks of my teaching career, when Mr Mac arrived at my school and asked me to take on a German tourist class as the teacher had let him down at the very last minute. Oh, what had I to lose? Did I not manage the forty-eight lively children in my class! How difficult could it be to teach a few adults?

That very evening I was asked to turn up and take the evening class. Weak-kneed, I arrived at the college and was shown my classroom where eighteen adults of mixed ages and sexes awaited me. I was introduced to them, and they were told how lucky they were to have me at such short notice. I sat down at the teacher's desk to greet them and to take the register. By now, not only were my knees shaking so badly that I could not stand up, but also my hands, so holding the pen was impossible. I gripped my hand and began my acting the part of an evening-class German teacher. As it was a tourist German class, I asked everyone where they wanted to go, and soon the ice was broken and I found my feet in more ways than one.

They were a great class and a great bunch of people. We had many laughs, and I even managed to teach them some German. The time passed all too quickly and it was time to go home. Suddenly, two gentlemen stood in front of me wanting to carry my books to the staff room door. I chuckled to myself and accepted their offer. They accompanied me outside, and we stood and chatted for quite a time before saying goodbye.

I could hardly wait for my next week's German lessons and prepared carefully to keep the class interested. I had to keep at least ten students to make the class viable. No problem—I kept all of sixteen for the next eight years, teaching them not only German language, but German customs, gave them German food recipes, and organized special German celebrations in the classroom, such as the celebration of Advent.

Back to the second night. At the end of the class, my two escorts waited for me again, and we chatted some more outside the college. One gentleman was from South Africa and wanted to know all about what to do and see in London. The other one lived locally and informed me that, like me, he only joined the class at the last moment, as he had originally wanted to learn Italian for the purpose of hitchhiking around Europe. We exchanged information between us and at the same time got to know each other a little more.

As it was October and getting very chilly in the evening, so the South African Gentleman suggested we should adjourn to have a coffee somewhere instead of catching cold. We all agreed and said we would do so the next week. When the next week's lesson was finished, the South African said that sadly he had to leave, and the other man replied that we should postpone the coffee for the following week. When the following week arrived, the South African couldn't make it after all, but suggested that the two of us should go on our own. Well, as the scene was set, the other man could hardly chicken out. We were seen off by our mutual friend, who waved us goodbye and saw us on our way. We never saw the gentleman again, but the coffee evenings continued every week and developed into romantic dates. The South African was our good fairy or guardian angel, and the other man was Charles, who became my beloved husband.

Courting, dating, visits to the theatre, opera, restaurants, naughty weekends away, and lovemaking soon became part of our life. I was in seventh heaven as I enjoyed my working life and at last had a man I could worship and who loved me in return. What could be better?

Charles had an old sports car, a Singer Le Mans, which he was very proud of and called her Prunella. We enjoyed our rides, but I nearly fell out of the car a few times because the doors only had a garden catch on them, having lost the real door locks a long time before. The passenger seat, too, was very precarious as it was damaged, and I often landed on my back but laughingly declared that it obviously was the position he liked to see me in best of all. We had great fun going about in Prunella and kept the roof down so the wind could ruffle my hair and caress my cheeks. How we laughed.

One weekend we actually went away to Surrey on the pretext of visiting Charles' friend. We did see him for a few moments, but stayed in a little hotel in Guildford to spend a naughty few days together. Charles was working for a government office and had to visit breweries and distilleries to proof the alcohol contents of their products. Thus, armed with illegal gin, which was more like neat spirit, and crisps, we prepared for our own seclusion in the hotel bedroom. We signed in as Mr and Mrs Smith and I wore his ring as a wedding band, as I did not want other people at breakfast to think that we were not an old married couple. How I blushed, whenever we met other residents.

There was not much sleeping, during those two perfect days, and lovemaking energy was kept alive by refreshing sips of gin.

The weekend passed very quickly, and we had to lie to Charles's mother and invent activities that we had done with the friends we were supposed to be visiting.

I met Charles's domineering mother and gentle stepfather as well as some of his friends like Peter and Joy to whom he introduced me as Doris. I kept looking about me for this girl named Doris and found out that it was me. Oh, we laughed a great deal and were so happy despite of Charles's mother making it clear that I was a foreigner and beneath him; he would be far better off with his English girlfriend (who shortly afterwards emigrated to Australia). Before long, Charles's mother threw him out of the family home, which was nothing to do with me but just a regular occurrence. Charles found lodgings nearby, and we continued our happy courtship for nine months.

Then, one night, we climbed up on top of Parliament hill often referred to as kite hill on Hampstead Heath. The twinkling lights of London were far beneath us, and a myriad of stars shone above with a full moon lighting up the entire scene. Suddenly, Charles dropped down on bended knee and asked me to become his wife. I was taken by surprise and whispered 'yes' and then shouted my affirmative over and over again, for the whole of London at our feet to hear and the benevolent, smiling moon to bear witness.

The moon and the stars smiled upon us, and I was the happiest person on earth, promising to be the best of wives and partners and to care and look after him as no one had ever been looked after before or since. I would be a whore in the bedroom, a perfect housewife, a mothering soul, a fun companion, and a social secretary. In fact promised him all this so as to be the perfect wife.

The next day, we scoured the second-hand jewellery shops in Hampstead for an engagement ring and found an unusual cat's-eye ring in a gold antique setting. Charles went to tell his mother and bought a huge bouquet of flowers for her. He never got closer than the front door but managed to tell her the news. She threw the flowers at him and screamed for him never to darken her doorstep again.

Evening classes had finished by then and my teaching career had progressed very well. I felt proud of my achievements and was ready to cope with anything.

I phoned my mother who was happy for me but said she was too busy to come to any wedding, so I should not include her in any wedding plans. Charles's mother too wanted to have nothing to do with us. We tried not to be upset at all this thoughtlessness and desperately wanted to share our joy with our families. However we continued to walk on air and plan a glittering future together.

Friends were happy for us, and nothing in this world could possibly darken our future together. I had met my soul mate and worshipped and loved him beyond any words that could possibly describe my feelings.

Charles told me of his childhood and the sad life that he had without his father, who had died of multiple sclerosis when Charles was only five years old. His mother had a hard time to raise him and would accept no help from the Freemasons, to which her husband had belonged. She allowed no charity to help educate her son. He did manage to get a place at the Haberdasher's School in Islington and was a very promising pupil. Like me, he was prevented from entering the university because his mother would not accept any grants, thinking of them as another form of charity. So he entered the Civil Service instead, as he had to help support his mother. He could never entertain friends at his house and longed for an open door approach to his home. I promised him we would do all that and catch up with all the things that he felt he had missed out on.

His mother, at the time had various 'boyfriends'—healers, members of the Spiritual Society, and others. One was called William, a widower, she had married a few years before I met Charles. So now Charles was free of having to care for her but continued living at home until he was thrown out of the family home over and over again. He would take a room somewhere, and before long, his mother asked him to move back home, as she did not want to lose control over him.

Well at this precise time, he had been thrown out again and was living near my flat. We saw each other every day and he only went back to his room to sleep. I learnt how to cook his favourite meals, and we cuddled together on my single bed. My body seemed on fire, my breathing fast and shallow, and I was wet all over. I did not understand these symptoms that overtook me whenever he was near, so I phone my friend Iris for advice and information. She enjoyed enlightening me.

After nine months, we decided to plan our wedding. As my mother said she felt unable to come to the UK because of her work and Charles's mother wanted nothing to do with us, we enquired about getting married in Paris, but were told that either we had to be resident there or I had to be in the family way. We could not meet either requirement, so we planned a wedding during my half term holiday in London. Charles and I went to town to buy a wedding ring and found a jeweller in Oxford Street who was delighted to be able to help us. He said Charles reminded him of James Mason, and joked with us and then gave us a discount for making his day. Alas, when we went to find our car, we realized that the car had been towed away and had to spend our discount loot on retrieving the car out of the pound.

My college friend Barbara on hearing my news offered us a Cornish cottage as a honeymoon resort, and as we had very few friends at the time and even less money, we planned a very simple wedding at the Wood Green registry office. Oh, where was my dream of a white wedding with me floating down the aisle looking beautiful and being surrounded by friends and family? As always, I tried to see sense and do without the frills. After all, was it not more important to marry the man of my dreams than to worry about flippant things?

Soon the wedding day was set, and I scoured the shops for something to wear. At least let me find something white and look at least a little like a blushing bride. The Wallace fashion shop provided me with a little, short, white dress and the haberdashers had a suitable rose headgear to wear for this occasion. I felt good.

Out of the blue, a day or so before the wedding, Charles's mother phoned and demanded his presence. She said her dead husband, Charles's father, had appeared to her and told her that she must swallow all her pride and had to come to the wedding. No one could have told her about the wedding as only a couple of friends knew and they were unknown to her. Whether the dead husband had appeared or not seemed unimportant. We were pleased that she would come, whatever the reason.

She then asked about arrangements for the wedding, who would attend and what plans had been made. She demanded who would collect her by car in order to take her to the wedding. Charles said he would do the honour himself and told me to take the bus instead.

I had invited my friend Christa's sister, who was at that time living and working in London in order to learn English, and also invited Charles's oldest friends, Peter and Joy, with whom he spent so many happy days in the Young Conservative Clubs. I also invited Brenda, the sister of his other friend who was away at that time. They were all shocked that Charles had left me to my own devices and had not even bought me some flowers, so they showered me with carnations and garden roses. I now looked the picture of a bride and was not put off going by double decker bus to get married. My friend Barbara and her husband would come too, as did Mr and Mrs Willis. I was not alone and glowed with happiness to become the wife of my beloved Charles.

The night before the wedding I stood naked, before my mirror and took stock of what I saw. There I was, a girl of 5'5 in height, with a large 34 DD bust, which had always troubled me for being so big. I always stood with my hands folded across my chest to hide this phenomenon, as I was so ashamed. My ears—the Bendiner ears—stood out from my head, and I always had to hold them back with strands of hair or hide them by wearing a long bob. Hilde and Sophie called me fat. What on earth did Charles see in me? Would he always love me as I would love him?

I put on my dressing gown, made a hot bedtime drink to calm me and continued my musing. Like all young girls, I had dreamt of floating down the aisle of some beautiful church in a billowing, white wedding gown—veil and all. The church would be decorated with fragrant flowers and the congregation would sing lovely hymns that sounded like a choir of angels celebrating my happiness. I would arrive in a garlanded, white Roll Royce and would be welcomed by all my loving family and friends, and Charles would stand tall and handsome that he was, at the altar, waiting for me to make me his own. Surely this is God's greatest gift to mankind—this happy union.

Well, all this dreaming would not do as it would never happen. One thing however was sure—I would become Charles's wife on the morrow and live happily ever after. What more could I wish for. The rest was unnecessary. The next day would be the most brilliant day in my life!

The dawned bright and sunny, and I dressed for my wedding. I boarded the bus to the registry office. I met all our friends there and awaited Charles and his parents to arrive.

The registry office wedding was nicely decorated with flowers, and we were made welcome. When I was asked whether I would take 'Charles David William' for my husband, I was startled. I only wanted Charles and not three other men. Silly me, I had never heard all his Christian names before, and Charles hastily pointed to himself. Relieved, I recovered and vowed to look after him in sickness and in health, for richer and poorer, till death do us part.

The wedding went off well and a photographer, who just happened to be present, marked the occasion with suitable photographs. Crisps, Madeira cake, and some African sherry was served in my little flat as a wedding repast. Charles's mother was furious and said she had never been so insulted, so she stormed off, throwing two dressing gowns at us as a wedding present. I had never been to a wedding and had no idea of what she had expected.

Our other guests smiled and wished us well as we left to go to Cornwall on our honeymoon.

We stopped in Salisbury overnight and looked for a little hotel to spend our first night together as husband and wife. There was no wedding supper or consummation of the marriage as we were far too tired, emotionally and physically. The next day, we continued our car journey to St Agnes in Cornwall. I felt St Agnes was a good omen to start off married life, for was not my Aunt Agnes my favourite Aunt and mother of my cousin Schorsch?

The cottage, a real Cornish, stone, farm cottage, down a little country lane, was very picturesque but primitive to the last degree. There was no furniture anywhere and only a camping stove to cook on. The water supply was outside the front door, both for washing, cooking, etc. Upstairs in the bedroom were two camp beds, which we tied together to serve as our nuptial couch. The toilet was an outhouse at the bottom of a field full of stinging nettles. We were undeterred and very happy and had a wonderful week exploring the countryside. We had glorious weather and enjoyed lying on the sandy beach and basking in each other's love. A perfect start to our life together.

Please God we would always be as happy as we were then.

We returned to London glowing with pride and happiness. We started our married life in my little flat on a single bed and infected everyone who knew us with our newfound happiness and joy.

I had realized my wildest dream and began my fairy tale life with a man I adored.

Chapter 16

Let's make our dream reality!

Every morning I would wake, and the song 'I 'm in love, I'm in love, I'm in love with a wonderful man' would immediately spring to mind.

The honeymoon being over, we settled down to married life in my little bedroom, with a small single, two foot six inch bed. Not the most comfortable, when two people have to sleep in it all night, but I could not throw my lodgers out, as they were just about to finish their teacher's training. Audrey was still waiting for her body to abort the dead infant—not a time to find themselves homeless.

Charles and I were very happy that living and sleeping so closely together was no hardship at all, but a bonus.

I was determined to be the best wife ever, a wonderful housekeeper, a remarkable and loving mother, a fantastic cook (for they do say that the way to a man's heart, is through his stomach), a generous and welcoming hostess at parties, and to boot all, an exciting whore in the bedroom. This will be my dowry, wrapped up as a special life present, tied in a golden ribbon and sprinkled in fairy dust with the blessings of all good fairies.

I had this idea that as a wife, I had to be responsible for all household duties, mothering, and the bringing up of the children. I had to serve my husband in every way I could. Where those ideas came from I do not know, as I had never lived with a male member in our household, and my mother certainly did not provide me with a role model. Perhaps I was once again influenced by Mr Shakespeare's *The Taming of the Shrew*.

> Thy husband is thy lord, thy life, thy keeper,
>
> Thy head, thy sovereign; one that cares for thee,
>
> And for thy maintenance commits his body
>
> To painful labour, both by sea and land.
>
> To watch the night in storms, the day in cold,
>
> While thou liest warm at home, secure and safe
>
> And craves no other tribute at thy hands
>
> But love, fair looks and true obedience
>
> Too little payment for so great a debt.

I really believed that I should comply with those thoughts, although nowadays the very idea would be foreign to women, who stand as equals in their partnerships. Freedom of speech, equal rights, and equal pay have been fought for and achieved. So how come I still believed that I had to be there for my husband in every way and serve him as best as I can? Well, I intended to and carry out what I believed was right for me.

Would I succeed or would life toss me around like a shattered straw in the wind, as it has in the past?

My childhood had been a very happy one, especially my Bavarian interludes. I did find that I had to fight for affection and attention from my nearest and dearest. Would I have to continue to prove myself? I was still not sure who I was—German, British, Jewish, or Catholic—but all that did not seem to matter any more. I was the wife of a fabulous man and would do anything and everything to make my marriage a success and make him proud of me.

Time passed as if in a dream. We lived in my little flat, but as the months went by, we thought it was time to try and buy a house, as we were both working and thought therefore that it would be easier to get a mortgage. We knew that we would be hard up but it was better that we pay money towards the value of the house rather than into a landlord's pocket. Discussing this with Mr and Mrs Willis, one day, they told us of their friend's sister, who had been taken ill and had to sell her house in Crouch End. As it was rather old fashioned and urgently needed some TLC, the price would reflect the work that needed to be done. Eagerly we went to view the property and were absolutely thrilled with everything we saw. It was a terraced house, high on a hill with views onto Alexander Palace. We were informed that that was the highest place west of the Urals in Russia. That however did not impress us too much. We just wanted that lovely house to be ours. It was on three floors with three bedrooms, bathroom, sitting room, dining room, kitchen, and scullery. In the attic were two more rooms that could be made habitable and thus bring us an income. Charles was a very handy man and had lots of ideas of how to renovate the house. As a special bonus, the house was fully furnished and contained some beautiful, old furniture. How lucky can one get?

We set to, to remodel the house and modernize it throughout. We moved the sitting room up into the first floor as this had such a fantastic view and made an extra bedroom downstairs, which, together with the dining room, that we converted into a sitting room and could then be let thus helping us pay off the mortgage. The garden was small but plenty large enough for our needs.

When Audrey and Colin saw the house, they immediately rented the downstairs rooms and made their home with us.

Before long the house was as good as new with central heating, bright colours, and all mod cons. I no longer had to get up and light fires in the grate and could enjoy hot water on tap. We tried to get a special warm terracotta colour to paint the living room, but as we could not find one to suit us, we mixed the colours ourselves and added cocoa powder to create the right effect. Soon, too, the garden was tamed, and we could enjoy the rewards of our labours by eating in the garden and sunbathing, weather permitting.

Earlier that year, before our wedding, I had promised the Highgate family to be their nanny while they went on holiday to Italy. I knew the children so well, and felt I had to keep my promise. Charles, too, persuaded me to go. After all, it was only for two weeks, and we had a lifetime together. I took pictures of Charles with me and a special little cartoon that he drew for me. This would be my contact with him.

My mother wrote that she, too, would be on holiday in Italy during my sojourn there and, as it was not too far from where we were staying, suggested that I visit her and my sister when I had some time off. Easier said than done, for as the family paid for everything, they expected me to be available night and day to look after the children.

However they relented and gave me three days off. I had to travel by train to Rimini and meet my family there. Oh, I had so much to tell my mother: about the wedding, our house, and our life in London. I sat in the train and the wheels kept chanting 'soon you'll see them; soon you'll tell them; soon you can hug them'. Sitting in my own reverie, I did not at first notice that the compartment had become empty of people and that the ticket conductor had sat down next to me. Before long, he started to make advances to me, and I had quite a job to fend him off with my limited Italian.

'Look,' I said pointing to my shiny, new wedding band, 'I am a married woman.' He then showed me his ring and stated that he too was married. In desperation, I said that I had three children but once again he topped it by proudly stating that he had three children. Just as I was getting really hot under the collar, we stopped at a station and more passengers came aboard, and I was saved by the bell, or to be correct, by the whistle.

Soon, I arrived at my destination, and I spent a great time together with my mother and sister. It was a lovely interlude.

Time passed, and I was back in Charles's arms.

Charles was still very keen to hitchhike to Greece, so with the extra money earned by me, we decided to take a three-week holiday and try our luck. It was a wonderful trip, and we met many kind and interesting people.

We started our hitchhiking by getting a lift in what looked like a Black Maria: an HM Customs and Excise van, in which colleagues of Charles took us on the first lap to Southend.

Travelling across Belgium, we left our passports in the car giving us a lift, but as it was noticed by the driver, we soon retrieved them and were more careful in the future. Germany was lovely, and we found great campsites there as we did Italy. A short boat journey across the Adriatic saw us into Greece, and we had our first tiff, which did not last too long, on the boat.

One lovely day, we met an older American couple, who spoke no Greek and drew everything that they wanted to ask. Easy for them, as the husband was a famous artist and even painted the presidents. We stayed in touch with them for many years.

We visited Olympia, and wandered around the ancient site, fascinated. I wanted to know where the Olympic flame was lit whenever Olympic Games took place somewhere in the world. I drew a picture of the lighting of the flame. I even tried to act out being a torchbearer and ran around the place. After much laughter, someone understood and showed us where to go and I had a photo taken of me lighting the imaginary torch. It was very hot in Olympia, but the place was built in such a way that a gentle breeze blew wherever we went. What clever builders the ancient Greeks were.

At another time, while trying to shop in remote villages where no one spoke English, we, speaking no Greek, had to improvise by pointing to different cheeses and said *tiri-tiri*, (cheese) and make sounds like 'ochi moo, moo' and 'meeh, meeh' and put our fingers to the head to represent horns. Everyone was most amused and doubled up with laughter, but we got what we wanted.

On one Greek island, we sat on the beach dabbling our toes in the sea while we were served dinner at a table right on the sea edge. It was easy to order the food, as the waiter took us into the kitchen, lifted all the lids off the saucepans, and let us taste to see what we wanted. We had a fantastic meal just as the sun was beginning to set and drop into the sea. The meal was complemented by delicious, cool wine.

Journeying on, we reached Athens, which was stunning with all the Greek temples and of course the Pantheon and the Acropolis, where we watched a Greek play by full moon and a bright starry sky above us. I understood only yes and no, but that did not matter, as we could follow the action.

Visiting the Corinth canal was quite something, and I wondered how on earth ships could sail through the narrow sea, crowded by very steep sides on either bank. The monastery of Meteora left great impressions on both of us. It is perched high on a perilous mountain, and it left us breathless in more than one way after climbing the steep, numerous steps, carved roughly inside the mountain. Food and other necessities were hauled up in a net on the outside wall. The monks were very hospitable, and offered us rainwater out of butts to drink and Turkish delight to eat, while giving us a short lecture about their history. A very spectacular visit.

On our return journey, we camped high on a mountain in Austria, and it was there that our first child was conceived. What a fantastically, beautiful place to begin a new life—may he or she be doubly blessed.

Before I became too big with child, I persuaded Charles to come skiing to Austria with me. My mother would be on holiday there, and they could at last meet. We left a very cold London that was deep in snow to arrive at a snowless Austria. It was wonderful to see Charles and my mother get on so well. Charles tried out all his German knowledge and soon was ordering the wine in fluent German. Much to everyone's amusement, he asked the waiter to bring some 'Virgin's Milk' and demanded to taste it first. *Liebfraumilch* never tasted the same again. Perhaps I was not as good a German teacher as people made out.

Christmas had arrived, and we attended midnight mass in a very cold church, huddling around electric fires, but we sang lustily and with gusto, even though we did not know the words, and soon warmed up. As if by magic on leaving the church we found that the snow had arrived, and by morning, everything was clad in white. Skiing could start, although not for me. I sat in the chairlift and was taken high up the mountains to meet my skiers. The forest below me was so silent and everything, the trees and the ground below, glistened silvery in the morning sun. I just held my breath and marvelled at God's creation. I was so happy to see Charles and my mother together—the two people I loved more than anything in the world. The fun over, we parted once again with promises from my mother of an early visit to London.

I continued work up to the last moment of my pregnancy, and we were both delighted when I was able to hand the newly born son to Charles. How proud he was to be a daddy. We called the baby Richard Paul, after his father, and soon started planning another baby, although I had a hard time giving birth and had to have a forceps delivery. I felt so lonely during the delivery, as fathers were not allowed to stay with their wives. I cried for my mother as I wanted her to reassure me and be there for this monumental event. Alas no, the only person in attendance was Miss Cruelty in person, a disgruntled mid-wife. When Charles arrived after my twelve hours of hard labour, all was forgotten, and I bathed in his pride and love. Even Charles's mother was pleased with her grandson, who she saw shortly after the birth, having been yet again sent by the spirit of her dead husband and told that she had to make up the rift between her and her son.

I had to give up work and planned to let the attic rooms to my friend Gordon and his newly wed wife. I also registered with the Nursery Nurses Bureau in order to take in children that needed short—term care. First, we took Charles's mother and William for a holiday to Spain, as soon as Richard was three months old. The vacation was not without problems and on return to the UK, Charles's mother once again ostracised her son. However, our life went on happily, and I added an Austrian au-pair to our household as well as a little boy, Sherif, of one year, whose parents were doctors and had to study for further exams in London. He was a real sweetie. I also worked part time for two days a week at my old school, helping out as they had staff shortages. I did however insist that baby Richard came too, and that worked out very well. He was such a good baby.

I had previously joined the Mountview Theatre club and took part in one or two plays and persuaded Charles to join me in this venture. It was a very happy club, and as my family grew, so did the number of our friends and we all had same age children who met frequently at club happenings.

Before long, the second baby was on the way, and I was deliriously happy and Charles was so very proud. Sadly that did not stop him from making advances to other women, in particular to a certain lady at the club who he found very sexy. I found them cuddling and kissing at one of the theatre cast parties, when I was nine months pregnant and felt like a colossal beached whale. I felt very shocked and upset but never said anything, although many people noticed and thought Charles was out of order. What does one do under these circumstances: make a fuss or let sleeping dogs lie and hope the whole affair would thus blow over? I chose the latter, never being one who could be confrontational.

My labour pains with our second child started when Charles had to perform in a play, and not wanting to worry him, I pretended all was well and served him his supper between collapsing in the kitchen while the contractions lasted. I tried to persuade him to leave early and have a drink in the bar with his friends. No luck. A last he left, and I tried to drive myself to hospital but the pains came too fast so I called a nearby friend to give me a lift. When the play was over, Charles was brought to the hospital to meet his second son, Tim. What a lovely family we had. Even my mother came over from Germany to meet them both, although she thought she was too young to be a granny at fifty-six.

To make Charles's wish come true, to keep an open house, and have many friends drop by, as well as having many parties, I did my best to make his dream became reality and thus we had a very busy social life.

We also went out regularly to cinemas and theatres, treating ourselves with a steak and kidney pie with daddy's sauce, bought on the way home from a kiosk under the Holloway arches. Yum, yum.

I discovered that Charles was a very able and talented cartoon artist and tried to encourage him to sell his work. He however did not believe in himself, so I went to all the newspapers in Fleet Street to show the art editors his work. They were impressed, but only one paper actually bought his work and asked for more. They made certain suggestions on how to improve his work, but Charles would not listen and left off drawing any more cartoons. I was so sad.

Being a bright and very personable young man, Charles found promotion by joining the Home Office team, dealing with drug prevention. I was so proud of him. He was one of the youngest to get that promotion. When he had to be away from home, to travel around the South of England, which was his patch, and the occasions permitted, we all became camp followers and travelled with him to various parts of the country and stayed in B and B places, so that we could be together.

A little mongrel dog that we named Cindy (short for Cinderella, as she had to stay in a pet shop alone over Christmas) soon joined our family. I was always afraid of dogs—even this little puppy, when she barked at me, due to the fact that I was bitten when a small child. I did not want our children to be afraid of animals and encouraged pets in the house. Soon, we added a cat to our tribe as well.

Richard adored his little baby brother, and as he could not pronounce his name, called him Ricky. That name stuck with him for many years. In the mornings, before we were awake, Richard would go to his brother's room and play with him. One morning, Richard came into out bedroom with hands covered in red—blood, we thought.

Oh my God, he has murdered his baby brother!

To our great relief he had done no such thing, but thinking the baby was hungry, fed him red paint as well as white paint that he took to be cream. Charles had been decorating and had left his tools around the room, and Richard had put them to good use, or so he thought.

Once Richard was three and a half and Ricky eighteen months old, I took the boys to Germany for a short holiday. We travelled by plane, and as the cheapest flight only took us to Dusseldorf, my mother said she would meet us there. On arrival with my boys, there was no one waiting, and we had to spend the night somewhere. A kindly official opened a room for us, a sort of waiting room, where we could spend the night and continue our journey the next day. I telephoned my new arrival time and was then met by a relieved mother in Frankfurt. We had a great time in Germany and even travelled down to Bavaria to visit my grandmother. Proudly, I showed off my two little boys and showed photos of Charles and our house. My joy was complete, when, again out of the blue, my cousin Schorsch arrived. He seemed to sense my presence and cycled thirty miles in order to see me. This happened at various times during my future visits to Germany and could never be explained. He was just there.

Our next holiday was camping in Italy by the Adriatic. The boys loved their camping life. They enjoyed playing in the warm sea and building sand castles in the fine, golden sand. I made them have their afternoon nap lying on a blanket and being sung to sleep by the murmur of the sea and the gentle caressing winds. We also visited Venice and other places of interest before driving back to the UK.

One day I had a great surprise, as my mother wrote that she and my Aunt Emmi from Bavaria would come to visit us. I was greatly excited and planned all sorts of sightseeing trips for them. I was determined that their stay would be memorable.

At that time we only had black and white television, but my aunt was enthralled with it. However, one day, as we were strolling through Soho, we came upon a window display with back projection showing a colour film. We told my aunt that it was colour television, and she just could not stop marvelling at this modern innovation. Oh, we did have such fun and I was sorry when they returned home.

Being at home, I often watched daytime television but found that it was very limiting as there were great gaps in screening shows. I had the idea of presenting special programmes for young children and wrote to the BBC setting out my ideas and giving various story lines, how to make things with paper and cardboard, songs and nursery games. I wrote that as I was a trained teacher, I would be very happy to present these shows during TV dead time and would be prepared to come up to London to discuss it all. All I received as an answer was that there were no plans to show anything along these lines. Years later all my ideas were being produced in *Blue Peter*. Well, that's life!

In London, houses were soaring in price, and we thought it best to move while we could make some money on our property and move to a better and leafier part of North London. We found a beautiful semi-detached house in Woodside Park. It had a very long garden and bordered onto a stream. The outlook was onto a field. Yet it was only five minutes' walk away from Woodside Park Underground station. We arranged the move with a day in hand to clean the new house so that everything could be moved into place straight away. I planned everything to the last detail, as I was pregnant again and needed to be organized. We still had our au-pair, but the little doctors' boy had left us. Audrey and Colin as well as Gordon and his wife had just moved on by then, so there were no complications.

Charles wanted a house warming-party the same day, so I had made a gallon of Bolognese sauce and cooked spaghetti, enough to feed an army, and made garlic bread. All this was done the night before the move and carefully transported. Cold beers crowned the evening. Many friends, mainly from the theatre club, came to wish us well. We had a lovely evening to start off life in our new house.

I was eight months pregnant and very large at that. I was trying to cook on a small camping stove, as we had no gas or electricity during the building work in progress. At last all was completed and another party followed to celebrate the completion of a task well done.

Number three son, Brian, was born shortly afterwards and to crown things, the dog Cindy had puppies as she had escaped while being on heat. Our house was full to the brim, and we were all very happy. Life was exciting and full of fun.

There were very few nursery schools, so I decided to run my own using part of our house. The necessary permission and inspections followed, and soon I had eight children attending every morning. A new au-pair had arrived, so I had plenty of help. Wonderful Charles built a climbing frame, a sand pit, and a terrace where the children could play.

Charles was still with the Home Office and enjoyed his job that was very interesting. He still had to be away from home at times, and I missed him terribly. I loved the guy more and more as time went by. I used to sit on his lap and wanted to merge with him, body and soul, so that there would be only one entity. I made him promise never to leave me and let me die before him as I could not live without him. We went everywhere together and held hands as we walked. We would even stop and kiss there and then in the High Road, when shopping, as I was overwhelmed with my love for him.

Oh, they were such happy times.

Charles continued to play at the theatre club, especially in the Old Tyme Music Hall, and I would take all the children to the performances and proudly watch and admire him. The boys got to know all the Music Hall songs and joined in the singing all the choruses.

Holidays were plentiful and varied. We camped in a small tent, until we could afford a bigger one, which made the wet days easier for the children.

Charles had made friends with a handyman/builder when he helped renovating our house and the two of them now set up a weekend whistle, decorating other peoples' flats and houses in order to earn some more cash. He and Dave really enjoyed their working time together. They learnt together to do all different kinds of jobs. When they accidentally smeared paint on the expensive carpets, they solved the problem by shaving the offending parts and no-one was the wiser. I would bring them lunch or some refreshment and 'oversee' the work in progress.

To make ends meet and money to go farther, I would go along to Chapel Market in Islington, just before closing time and get reduced meat, broken biscuits, and dented tins of vegetable and fruit. At Christmas, I would go on Christmas Eve and get really cheap chickens and turkeys, as well as Christmas trees. Laden with our booty, we joyfully went home and were never short of any food or special treats.

My kindergarten group thrived, and I added part-time work in a local school twice a week in the afternoon while the children slept. Neighbours too were friendly and often came to visit us. One of our neighbours turned out to be Spike Milligan and his family. The youngest child, Jane, came and joined my nursery and grew up with my boys. Her mother, Paddy, and I became great friends and spent much time together. One day Paddy had to rush home to meet her masseur and suggested me joining her. I was so embarrassed even to contemplate undressing and being massaged by a young man, however as always I reasoned with myself and told myself that all this was normal to him and he would not think anything of it. So I agreed to ask the young man over to my house when he had finished massaging Paddy. I suffered all my life with bad migraines and varicose veins, so I thought this might help.

Peter was a charming man and soon became a regular visitor once a week. He stayed to supper and became a friend. I was so interested in his skills that I questioned him at length until he suggested that I took a course at his old college. I could study all the physiology by correspondence and then attend weekend courses to learn the practical approach. These were held in a hotel in London, so I discussed all this proposal with Charles and decided to give it a go. Well, I thought this was the nearest that I would come to being a doctor and therefore threw myself into the studies, progressing from the standard to the advanced courses. I loved it and practised on all the family.

Peter was studying to be an osteopath, and when he completed his course, his weekly sessions of massage came to an abrupt halt. I took on some of his patients, hoping to be as good as he was.

I managed to save some money and presented Charles with a surprise present: a caravan. I furbished it with everything that was needed—cutlery, china, pots and pans, sleeping bags, and first-aid kit—all ready at all times to go off on holiday. Our tent would serve as extra space for the boys. Now we could have holidays in style, regardless of the weather. We travelled far and wide, seeking out new places and sandy beaches. I made sandwiches to order in the car while travelling and once we fed the '5000' we sang, told jokes, and played guessing games.

Mad that I was, I had the notion of getting a pony for the children, and as our quarter of an acre garden was very long with an orchard and a stream at the end of it, I nagged Charles until he at last gave in. He built a stable, and we bought a pony, that we called Patch. I had done the necessary research by asking the council whether it was permissible to keep a pony in the garden. I also checked with the neighbours. The boys could now learn riding and had great fun with the horse. I went out to a local riding stable and learnt how to ride (although I was terrified, not knowing which end was more dangerous to me—the biting or the kicking end). I also received advice on horse keeping and invited the teacher to come and give the boys some necessary instruction on riding and horse care.

The pony tried to escape several times and was found either nearby knocking over dustbins or actually having been caught by the police and taken to the horse pound in a nearby farm. Well we made our name in the neighbourhood!

The children were growing up fast. Tim was attending the nursery school next to the primary school. The head was a real Tartar, and everyone was afraid of her. One day, I was shopping with little Brian in our busy High Street, when suddenly my little two-year-old had disappeared. I was frantic with worry. Where was he? I looked into the road but as there had been no accident and there was no blood to be seen, I hurried from shop to shop, searching for him. I looked at the time and found that I was going to be late for collecting Tim and really panicked. What was I to do? I was afraid of the head and did not want my little boy punished for my lateness; on the other hand, I could not leave the High Road while Brian was missing. I was quite beside myself and did not know what to do. Suddenly, a lady came out of Woolworth carrying my baby boy. He wanted to buy sweets so he wandered off, still carrying the Smith's bag in his hand. The lady made the deduction that I had to be in Smith's so she came to find me. I could have hugged her and did not know how to thank her. Relieved, we both went to collect Tim and all was well.

Life continued, and I had another birthday approaching. I had more than I wanted, and hence the only wish to remain unfulfilled was a fourth baby.

When Brian, our youngest son, was 4, our long-awaited daughter Stephanie arrived, to everyone's great joy. The boys were so proud of their wee sister, and Charles was over the moon to have a little girl, as indeed I was too. I found that my cup of happiness was indeed overflowing. While still in the maternity wing of the hospital, I kept checking under her nappy to make sure she was a girl. Charles's mother came to stay in our house, so I begged the nurses to keep me in hospital the full time of ten days instead of sending me home after twenty-four hours. I wanted to enjoy my little girl and have her all to myself for a little time. Anyway, I wanted to recover before having to look after Charles's mother and having to meet all her numerous demands.

I breast fed all my babies and wished Miss Halliday from the College could see me. All the babies thrived, but I could only manage to feed them for three months, as they all made by breasts sore, bleeding, and extremely painful. I always had to grit my teeth when starting breast-feeding because of the pain. Afterwards, I would sit and cuddle them and sing to them. I would often sit for an hour with each of the babies, rock them in my rocking chair, and sing all sorts of songs to them. These songs and melodies would bubble out of my head, be they German, Czech, or Russian children's songs, German and English folk songs, snippets from operas or operettas, pop songs of the time, and even German marching songs that the German army had so happily sung as they marched through the parks of Prague. I also quoted Shakespeare and various poems, both from my childhood and from school in Reading. Often, I had no idea where the songs and poems came from or how I had remembered them. The babies seemed happy and content and safely in my arms would fall asleep. I really relished those times.

There were so many children without parents and Charles had always wanted a football team of children, so I thought we should pay back something for being so happy and so very lucky. I had a great house, four fantastic children, cats, dogs, and even a pony in the garden for the children to ride, but most of all I had a wonderful husband whom I loved beyond life itself. Thus, we considered adopting two Vietnamese girls, but that was no longer possible, whereas there were many black, West Indian children urgently needing homes. The social services did not allow us to have the two girls, but at a later date, we welcomed, Cindy into our home.

She was a year younger than Stephanie, and the two little girls became great friends and have remained 'sisters' ever since.

I found Cindy difficult to cuddle and love as she pushed me away and preferred men to get close to. She had a father living in Camden. Her mother had died, suffering from schizophrenia. Her older brother had mental developmental problems and was in a home. She saw her family occasionally, but it was not always a happy meeting. However, we all loved her and she became part of our little family. At times, I felt like the wicked stepmother as I was angry that I could not get close to her.

My early Catholic religious training was never far from my mind, and I wanted to be a kind person, otherwise I would never get to heaven, sit on a fluffy cloud, and join the throng of angels playing sweet music. I did not want to be sent to purgatory to absolve my sins and certainly did not want to end in fiery hell for eternity. So please don't let me be wicked. Once, the children were in bed Charles and I could sometimes go out to have time to ourselves.

My morning nursery continued as before. The boys had both started at the local primary school and enjoyed their school life.

One day, I heard that a primary school was looking for a person to open and run a nursery class within the school, and I was invited to take on the new post. As long as I could take my present children attending my own nursery and if the parents wished it, I would be delighted to take the post. It was good to be working as part of a school again, and I decorated, cleaned, and furnished the place, which was a Nissen hut some way away from the main school. I made curtains for the windows, painted pictures on the windowpanes, and before long had twenty-five children to care for.

We had a morning and an afternoon class. At first, I was alone with them, and I shall never forget my need to go to the toilet and have a dozen children peering under the door, demanding my presence. Later, a nursery nurse was added to the unit. I worked there for two and a half years before moving to another primary school where I taught every afternoon, offering art, craft, and religious instruction to lively juniors. The school was on a rough estate, and some of the parents were well known troublemakers.

One day, when I reprimanded a boy, he stormed out, and I thought that he had gone to the toilet—but no, he had gone home. The first I knew about it was when an irate mother stormed into my class, swearing at me. I took her outside and commiserated with her for having to deal with a lively youngster. She became 'my best friend', much to the astonishment of the headmaster who knew the difficult customer.

The head too started to confide in me regarding various problems. One day, he told me all about his kidney stones and how he had to painfully pass them out through his penis. I was so embarrassed, as I was naive and did not know what to say.

Next, came a call from a local Catholic primary school to see if I could help out two afternoons a week. Never wanting to say no, Stephanie and I went to teach there for a spell.

One morning, while breast-feeding my little daughter in bed, I received a phone call from the boys' school asking whether I could come in and help out because a teacher was absent and they had no-one to take the class. I arrived with baby and soon became an institution at the school and was offered a full-time job to teach the reception class. I had never taught infants but thought *how difficult would that be?* I handed in my notice at the junior school, and my baby daughter and I started teaching at the new school. Stephanie became the school's and Education Office's mascot. I really enjoyed my teaching career, and as I had my daughter with me and the boys attending the same school, I felt everything was working out well. Charles, too, had changed jobs and worked in an office nearby, dealing with the government's newly introduced VAT. He could be at home early and did not have to travel any more.

I at last felt that I was successful as a mother, teacher, and wife.

CHAPTER 17

With a new job in the offing, I had to organize my life a little better.

Before I could take up the new post, I was asked by the Education Office to open a new reception class at another primary school that had problems with over subscription. Again, Stephanie and I set off to join another school and run a class in the canteen for a term—challenging but fun.

Then, I was at last free to take up my new job. I loved every moment of it, and Stephanie thrived with all the attention she was getting. During the lessons, she slept outside the classroom in her pram and when awoke would play on the floor with toys.

As a three year old, Stephanie went to the adjoining nursery school in the morning and then was with me at school in the afternoons. She learnt to read and write before I even realized it, as she was always with a group and joined in when she could. The boys had moved on to the junior department and were doing very well. They also joined the local Scout troop as cubs and later became Scouts. Their Scoutmaster was a lovely man, who became a firm family friend. Charles, being a good dad, helped out at the Scout troop and often went to 'Father and Sons' camps with the boys. They always returned home dirty and tired, having had great fun together.

Charles had changed his job to work locally at the new VAT office. He only had to travel five minutes to work and was very happy with his new post.

Lady Luck smiled upon us as developers wanted to buy our house, and they offered us a very good price, well above the normal house price. So, once again, we went house hunting and were very lucky to find a lovely Edwardian detached house in need of modernizing.

The new house was big and spacious with a large garden. We had an open aspect to the rear of the house onto the underground, but there was a large plot of land between us and the actual train rails. We were never aware of trains passing by.

Charles was in his element, remodelling the house. He divided the large bedrooms into two, so that each boy had his own bedroom. He designed and built bunk beds with the bed part at the top and a little study below the bed where we put desks and bookshelves. He built a wardrobe on the side. It was an ingenious design, and I wanted him to register and patent the design and market it, but he saw no future for it—pity, as it would have made us some money. Now of course one can find these bunks everywhere. Oh, Charles was so clever and gifted, and I wanted him to use his talents as I was so proud of him but could not persuade him to branch out. He was a great father and loved telling and making up exciting bedtime stories.

Before long our new house was ready. It had seven bedrooms and a large playroom in the attic. I continued to have au-pairs to help in the house and took in foreign students who wanted to learn English so as to supplement our income. By having other nationals living with us, I reckoned that it would broaden the minds of our children, who would learn about other customs. For quite a few years, we had Japanese students who were absolutely delightful.

We also had an Iranian girl who stayed with us some time and always delighted Stephanie and Cindy with belly dancing and me with Iranian cookery.

Living with all these students broadened all our outlooks and made life interesting. Up to that time, I had never seen Japanese or Chinese people, let alone Indian or Black people, and I was still the foreigner, alien. So not only did I earn some money this way but also made many friends from all over the world. Life was very rich and full of laughter.

Once the house was completely refurbished, we set about remodelling the garden. A put-up swimming pool was added. I had taken the boys to swimming lessons almost as soon as they could walk and continued a weekly lesson before school every Friday, so they were very able swimmers. In fact, as I had a couple of years before, I went swimming with them. When I was nine months pregnant and everyone worried that I would have the baby in the pool, I just laughed and said that it would be just another water birth.

We had apple trees, beans, and tomatoes growing in the garden.

With the garden established, Charles built another stable with a hayloft and created a fenced in paddock. Another pony found his way into our family. Not content with having two dogs and two cats, I added two geese, seven chickens, and two ducks to our menagerie. The children also had their rabbits, guinea pigs, a hamster, and even a garter snake as their own pets. I then added two goats to keep the pony company. I always wanted to live on a small holding so that the children would grow up with a love of animals but at the same time wanted city educational opportunities for them. Well, now I could provide them with both, and my beloved, long suffering husband reluctantly agreed as long as I did all the work. Feeding cost me nothing as I collected food from greengrocers, farms, and restaurants.

We lived the *Good Life* long before the TV programme came on the air, and harvested eggs, fruit and vegetables. The children all had their weekend tasks to help with the house and garden work.

Our au pair trained the pony and took her for walks. The boys, particularly Tim, enjoyed taking the goats for walks on a dog's lead. He dressed them in colourful vests and walked them in the park. People passing by did a double take when they looked again and saw the goats, having thought that they were dogs. The pony, when transported in our Volkswagen caravette, made passers-by look twice to see a horse travelling by car. The chickens scared me, and I had to use a broom to protect myself when feeding them. The ducks were sweet but messy, and the geese loved being cuddled by me and guarded our house better than any dog. Even the rabbit thought she was a dog and would make barking noises when someone approached the cage.

When feeding the animals, I had to be careful as the pony ate the goats' food, and the goats tried to eat the pony's food. Oh, we did have some fun watching all the animal antics.

When Wimbledon was on television, the pony would nose open the sliding doors and come into the house, stand in front of the television and watch the ball going from left to right. The geese tried to follow but were chased out by the dogs, who knew I did not want a mess in the house. On the whole all the animals got on very well and we had no trouble.

Even the snake, which was supposed to be kept in Tim's room, found its way downstairs, slithering this way and that way to join in the fun.

One night, I was woken by terrible screams coming from the horses' stable. I was terrified and tried unsuccessfully to wake Charles. I took the dogs outside with me to investigate. I found a terrified pony cowering in a corner of the stable and saw the goat with her throat ripped open. Scared that I was, I took both animals into our lean-to and made a bed for them. I also bandaged the goat's throat and calmed both animals.

Another time, I was woken by the geese crying out in the night, as they were caught napping when a fox appeared, but by banging on my window I managed to scare him off. I then shut my lovely geese away for the rest of the night.

The chickens were not so lucky, as I found seven headless birds lying in front of their chicken house.

The children and their friends would come to play and help as well. When they were tired of playing with the animals, they, unknown to me, would decide to make their own fireworks and 'bombs' and we had very close misses of explosions of all sorts.

I found an inexpensive outlet for clothing and school uniform helped a great deal. No one was in competition with rich peers.

Not enough to do what with a full time job at school, my 'little farm' and my expanding family, I took on the honorary job of being the secretary to the Barnet Borough Arts Council, and then chairman. I had never done any secretarial work before and found it a challenge hard to refuse. I remained as such for the next twenty years. It was very interesting, and I met many people. I had to be responsible for a large amount of money to be shared out amongst all the amateur arts societies in Barnet. There were concerts to arrange, drama festivals to organise, and exhibitions to mount as well as poetry readings and creative writing to be held. I tried to get the Council to provide us with an arts centre—alas, no.

Later, we even managed to get a full time arts officer appointed. I then had the idea of getting columns erected around the borough to serve as advertising space for our societies but was told they would be a safety hazard (however ten years later they erected them in the very spots I had chosen)

I became very proficient at speaking at large meetings (300 people or more), meeting with the mayor and various dignitaries as well as famous people. I even entertained Margaret Thatcher! Of course, wherever I went, my children and Charles would come too, and the mayor often held my baby daughter in his arms while I had to make a speech. Charles was always the life and soul of the party and encouraged me in every way when I organized special festivals in the borough, embracing all forms of art. We had pottery and sculpture being demonstrated in stores, huge, massed orchestral concerts in one of the cinemas, and numerous theatrical productions taking place all round the borough. There was a regular diary of events to publish and readings in libraries to organise. It was a very creative and entertaining time, but after twenty years, I decided to resign. Enough is enough.

I felt at the pinnacle of my life, with everything running smoothly for the erstwhile Orphan Annie. I could not have been happier, and my little family was thriving.

As the girls grew up, they joined the Brownies and Girl Guides and went camping, but they were not as enthusiastic as the boys.

Once the boys were old enough to learn a musical instrument, I encouraged them to join classes and then orchestras and bands. Richard first learnt the violin, the Suzuki method, and scratched away merrily on his instrument. Like me he never wanted to practice, but when he played in the orchestra would mark time during the hard bits and join in happily as soon as he could. I tried everything to make practice fun. Soon, Tim too joined his brother in having violin lessons. I was even invited onto television to share my experiences of the Suzuki method.

Later, in the junior school and secondary school Tim learned the trumpet, Brian the euphonium and trombone, and Richard changed from violin to tuba. Stephanie and Cindy learnt the tenor horn and trumpet, respectively. I joined them by learning the cornet and taking lessons from their teacher. We could now have our own brass band and play Christmas carols and music for other occasions. On holiday in Cornwall we would join the Silver Band and play marching through the streets of Wadebridge.

The boys joined the Barnet brass and wind band, which played to a very high standard, giving concerts at the Albert Hall and other venues. They had a great conductor who took them everywhere to play their music—even to Switzerland. Little Brian would play along professionals and then feel lost when they all disappeared to the pub, while he was too young. I was so proud of all my boys.

The girls did not like bands or orchestras and soon gave up learning their instruments. They preferred ballet, tap, and Scottish dancing instead and from going to one class a week, were soon attending on three nights a week, progressing through all their dance grades and reaching very high standards, with honours. I attended every class, and rather like Madam Defarge (*Tale of Two Cities*) would sit and knit endlessly through all their lessons and make jumpers for everyone—a double whammy. I was very proud of my girls.

Charles's mother had moved house several times during all this time. We all went and visited her often, bringing gifts and flowers. The children had to sit quietly, ask permission to go to the toilet and generally be seen but not heard. She always had a cake waiting for them and some pocket money for ice cream. She never offered to babysit, even when I was ill in hospital. Cuddling or making a fuss of them was not in her nature, so the children stayed remote and were always on their best behaviour. She never praised them but would often rave about neighbours' children and say how wonderful they were. I was really very sad about that as I so much wanted someone to spoil them and have fun with them.

My mother was no better, as she rarely came to England and then behaved just like a visitor. I remember Richard, when four years old, having had many problems with tonsillitis so that I took him to hospital for a tonsillectomy. I wanted nothing but the best for my little son. I took him to Elizabeth Garret Anderson Hospital, where I could be with him all the time. I needed my mother to stay with Tim at home, but she was not interested and left for Germany instead of staying a few days longer than she had planned. How disappointing for me. Charles and the au-pair looked after Tim instead while I remained with Richard. The operation went very well, and he amazed everyone by recovering very quickly, somersaulting around his cot, while the other children who had no parent with them, cried and whimpered.

All the children received ice cream after their ordeal, but Richard sighed and said 'Not ice cream again. Please, may I have cream crackers and cheese?'

The nurses searched the hospital and found his treat for him. Two days later, we were back at home. I missed my mother but had to get used to the idea that she just was not granny-like or the motherly type. Five days after the operation, Richard had a post-operative bleed and we had to rush him back to the hospital. It all looked more frightening than it really was and the next day all was well and he returned home. Quite an experience.

With no support from our immediate family, Charles and I built up a self-supporting unit and relied on no one. We were proud to be independent and were very happy with our family and zoo. We both worked hard but had lots of time for holidays with the children. We always took our caravan around the country but fed up with the wet summers decided to go to France. We found a lovely camping and caravanning place at Bois Soleil Royan near Bordeaux. It was a beautiful place, set amidst pine trees. Each area was separated by a tall hedge and had had its own water and power supply. We had plenty of room to put up our tent as well. We bought a little fridge and thus had all the comforts of home. The sandy beach was spacious, and the children loved it. There were shops and restaurants on the site and we made many friends. Charles became known as Monsieur le Playboy. We loved the place and returned there for quite a few years. Sometimes friends from London came to visit us and the big boys (Charles and Ron) would go, screwdriver in hand, and like mischievous children and take down interesting signs, to take home as souvenirs. How we laughed.

One night, we had a terrible storm, and suddenly a very wet and bedraggled Burford family arrived at the caravan door in the middle of the night to seek shelter, as they had been flooded out in their tent. I made up dry beds for them all. We then had a midnight feast of cocoa and biscuits. Charles slept through it all.

As we still had some money left over from our windfall from the developers we thought it a good idea to buy a holiday home in the UK. We looked around Wales, which we loved, and then Cornwall, where we were very lucky to find a lovely bungalow close to the beach in Polzeath. It had three bedrooms, a large sitting room, kitchen, and bathroom. There was a terrace overlooking the sea and a campsite, well below the bungalow, which was high on a hill. We had a front as well as a rear garden (with badgers!). There was also a large garage. The neighbours were lovely people and looked after our place when we were not there. I loved the place and thought that we were really very lucky to find it. We bought it there and then and had a holiday home that we could return to again and again. This now could become one endless holiday for the children as they could enjoy going back every holiday and just take up their activities, as if they never left, just as I had always done in going to Bavaria. They would get to know the people and discover new places to explore and play with the marching band.

Life was good and the 'man upstairs' must surely love us.

CHAPTER 18

WE ALL LOVED CORNWALL, AND every time we went there it seemed a continuation of the last time. That was exactly what I wanted for them as it reminded me of all my happy times in Bavaria and endless summers. We spend every holiday, half term, and Christmas there, often bringing the children's friends with us.

In summer there were beach picnics and beach bonfires when we cooked under the stars. The children collected seashells, flowers, and explored the life around the Cornish coast. We made friends with the locals and often went out fishing with them. At first we were paying customers but soon became part of the village life so that we were invited to come just for fun and fish for mackerels. Often Norman, who owned a boat, would come and wake us in the morning to invite us to go fishing. We jumped out of bed, soon dressed, made sandwiches, and were ready to leave. Sometimes, the sea was very rough and we 'fed the little fishes', being seasick. Sometimes, we even had to wear life jackets. Other times, we would all go skinny-dipping on a sheltered beach.

Charles also made friends with local fishermen and would go out with the fishing fleet, bringing back hundreds of fish for our freezer.

Charles had to return to London to work; he did not have long holidays. Eagerly, we awaited his return.

In the meantime, the boys and girls continued to enjoy their Cornish life. I encouraged them to take on little jobs such as selling ice cream in the kiosk or help in the local bookshop or stock shelves in the supermarket. Thus, they became part of the scene and were not looked upon as 'emroids' (a pain in the bottom) as visitors were often referred to.

The children all bought wet suits with their earnings as well as surf boards and learnt surfing, wind surfing, and belly surfing. They spent hours in the sea, and I would hoist a flag from a pole by the bungalow to call them in to their mealtimes. At other times, I would bring the food to them, and we would all enjoy a sandy picnic. Time passed very quickly, and when the holidays were over, we returned to London and awaited our next visit.

One special half-term holiday, it was Brian's turn to invite a friend down to Cornwall. Waiting for Charles to finish work, I prepared everything. I climbed up to the attic. Suddenly, the staircase slowly moved away from the doorway, just like a ship leaving its mooring. I then fell ten feet. I realized I must have broken something and called out for Richard (now fourteen). I examined my leg and found that it had immediately swollen up like a balloon and was already turning black and blue. I was in such pain. I tried to get up but was unable to do so. I asked him to call an ambulance.

Just as I was crawling to the bedroom, the phone rang, and it was Charles asking how things were progressing. I told Richard to say nothing about my fall but went to the phone to assure Charles that all was well but as I had a little accident, I was just taking myself to the hospital for a check-up and would see him later. A curt doctor sent me to the X-ray department and then pronounced me fit to walk home. I could not even stand on the leg and thought I would pass out any moment, so the doctor gave me crutches and muttered when I begged him for some painkillers. I had no money, no shoes, so how was I to get home? A taxi was called.

Richard was great helping me. It had always been my policy to acquaint all the children with doctors and hospitals and look at them as being friendly, interesting places. When I had to go into hospital for a varicose-vein operation, I gave Charles the wrong time for the operation so as not to worry him and pass his fears onto the children. Thus it came about that that he visited with all the tribe just as they wheeled me back into the ward, and I was still semi-conscious. On hearing their little voices, I shot upright and laughed and smiled, telling jokes and then dived under the bed to retrieve presents that I had brought with me for the children. Charles was so shocked that he made a hasty retreat, and I just fell back into my pillows and was out cold for another four hours. But it was worth it for the children to have no fear of doctors and hospitals.

When Charles came home, he carried me into the car and off we went to Cornwall. After a really painful night, I decided to visit the local hospital. As soon as the doctor saw me, he explained that I had completely smashed my heel and would not be able to walk for the next three to four months. A plaster cast would not help, so I just had to keep off the leg.

We still had a good holiday, and Charles carried me in and out of the car whenever we went out. Once back in London, I revisited the casualty department armed with a letter from the Cornish doctor. I found crutches were impossible because they slipped on wet flooring. I preferred to crawl or use my bottom for going up and down stairs. Trays with coffee I pushed along the floor using only half filled the cups in case of spillage. I asked for a Zimmer frame and then found that I was able to move about quite freely on my own. Charles's mother never popped in to see if she could help. She only lived five minutes from our house. Well, what could I expect? I became very adept at scooting around with shopping trolleys and somehow kept my boat afloat.

As promised, we kept an open house at all times. The children, too, had a wide social circle and were busy enjoying growing up.

Every morning at the infant school gates, I met a lady, named Margaret, with her son. It seemed that our boys were always a little late, and we got talking. That was when both Richard and Margaret's son, Mark, were five. Margaret, I, and the boys became firm friends and have remained so to this very day. I called Margaret my 'sister' as I had no close family nearby. We would talk and put the world to right. I was welcomed into the arms of her whole family, and as she lived nearby, I saw quite a lot of her.

One summer, while the boys were still little, we borrowed her in-law's caravan, which was in a caravan park on Mersey Island, near the sea's edge. It was a lovely place, and at that time there were not many people around. The boys would play by the sea, and Margaret and I would potter around the caravan, often still in our nightclothes. One day, a milkman called and was very surprised to see me in butch pyjamas and Margaret in a baby doll nighty. As the boys were nowhere to be seen, he thought we must be a pair of lesbian ladies—not something that was talked about much at that time. We giggled and made the most of that funny situation. We still laugh about it today.

Time has passed, but Margaret and I are still best friends, sharing in joy and grief. She is an honorary aunt to my children, and I even became godmother to one of hers. We are as close as ever, and I often wonder where I would be without her.

When the time came that the boys started to have girlfriends, I wanted Charles to make sure that they knew all about the birds and the bees, but he did not want to enlighten them so I made it my task to talk to them. The boys listened carefully and then said cheekily that it would be the girl's duty to take precautions, at which I became furious. They just laughed and said they were teasing me and knew all about sex from school and their mates. They would also try out various swear words on me when Charles was not about, and as I never knew what they meant, they delighted in enlightening me. We were all very close and there was nothing that they could not tell me. Of course, they had their own secret life, which they shared with their siblings that I knew nothing about. Smoking was tried out in their bedrooms so that we knew nothing about it.

By then, the children all had their own bikes and would go to the nearby park to play. I had warned them about strange men who would expose themselves and told them not to be frightened, but look away and say, 'Oh, put it away, Mister. Our horse has got a bigger one than that.'

School days were happy days, and I made sure that would stay so. When it came to their secondary education, I fought hard to get them into the best school and went to great lengths to achieve this. I never gave them the choice and refused to listen to what school their friends went. Nothing but the best was good enough for them. Music, scouting, guiding, and dance continued, and the boys became very proficient in all they did. School reports, too, were excellent and we could not ask for more.

Life became one continual holiday. Soon, we were back in Polzeath and continued our exploits. Sometimes there were visiting theatrical performances on the beach, while other times we would take the children into Wadebridge to the cinema. This was a little cinema and reminded me of our place in Bavaria. Once skateboarding became the fashion, the boys needed to be taken to the most adventurous skate boarding centres, otherwise they would skate down the steep hills that led into Polzeath, which I hated them doing because of all the traffic. Broken bones were soon seen to at the Bodmin hospital and off they went again. Oh yes, we got to know all the doctors and emergency places!

Visitors came and went all summer, and I had to cook and clean for them too.

I thought this happy time would never end. I loved Charles more as time went by and hated him being away from me. Not that all was roses—oh we had thorns, stormy weather, and real thunderstorms where Charles and I were concerned. He was not always easy to live with and became rather an emotional bully as the years went by. I dare say I was not all he dreamt of. Given time, these days would pass and when he refused to talk to any of us. That too passed as soon as visitors called to see us and he would be the life and soul of the party.

As the boys grew up and started to lock horns with the head of the herd, he would bang on the table with his fist, scream at them, and then refuse to speak with them for the next three weeks. I am afraid I was not very good at encouraging them to speak up for themselves, as Charles would get even angrier, and I made them keep peace by keeping quiet. They had each other to talk things over and even laugh at Charles' antics.

As time passed, Charles became more and more the emotional bully, and I would cower and become a doormat instead of standing up for myself. Mealtimes in particular became a nightmare for all of us. Charles would sit at the head of the table, bang his fist, and shout at all of us for what he thought to be bad table manners. He would direct his wroth especially at me, saying that no wonder the children had bad table manners as I encouraged them with my filthy Continental habits. I said nothing and let each occasion pass. Even when we had visitors, he would demand that they sit up, bosoms out, and hold their cutlery correctly and show their little finger. I was so embarrassed and Stephanie would always seek my hand under the table to comfort me. Still, all that would pass and soon he would again be the jovial character that we knew.

During those times I seemed to revert to my childhood fears, afraid to say anything in case I rocked the boat and then I would not be loved any more. I dared not stand up to my husband—*more shame on me*. Had I learnt nothing from my past?

His mother would visit infrequently, and I would polish the entire house till it shone like a new pin, shop for the best food, and cook and bake so that I would be the perfect hostess, but could never please her. I just could not win. I was and stayed Continental rubbish in her eyes. No wonder Charles could be so difficult at times.

I had always planned festive occasions, and birthdays and Christmases were very special in our house. Right from a very early age I put on special parties for the children with many surprises. Richard and Tim had a joined twenty-first birthday party, a dinner-jacket affair at our house, for which I cooked and baked. We had fifty guests, music, and dancing in the garden. It was a memorable occasion.

I tried to keep Christmas the way I remembered my German Christmases. No decorations would be put up until all the children were in bed. Then, Charles and I would play at being the Xmas angels and bring in the tree and decorate it as well as the rest of the house. The presents would be put under the tree for the next morning, when a little bell would sound calling everyone present to come downstairs and begin celebrations. Stockings would be hung up the night before, and I would fill those with fruits, biscuits, and sweets, as well as little toys. Charles would then have the task of hanging them at the bottom of their bed when they were all asleep. He would cut out little hoof—prints and spray them white, as if the reindeer had left their mark. He also had to eat the mince pies that the children had left out as well as drink the whisky meant for Father Christmas—no hardship there.

The next morning, we all attended church before settling down to opening presents.

There were huge piles of presents under the tree the next morning, and we sat for nearly two hours trying to open them all while we admired everybody's presents and eating Xmas pastries. Often my mother and Charles's mother and William would come and join us for Christmas. It was magical. We would sing carols, eat, drink, and generally be merry. Then came the silence for the Queen's speech, before having Christmas dinner, which I cooked: turkey, homemade Christmas pudding (with silver sixpences in it), and all the trimmings. Cold turkey sandwiches for supper in front of television completed the day. We all loved Christmas and its magic.

At Easter time, the Easter bunny came, and we all had Easter egg hunts. If we were in Cornwall during that time, the bunny had to come then and hopefully no hedgehog, badger, or other animals would eat the eggs before the children found them.

The tooth fairy in the guise of Charles appeared at regular times, leaving fairy dust behind to show that they had called. When VAT came in, Richard wrote a letter to the tooth fairy saying that the price had gone up and he was very sorry. We loved our magic moments and hoped that the children would remember them when they had a family.

One day, Charles had to go into hospital for a haemorrhoid operation. His mother and the boys came to visit. The conversation came round to the family history, when she suddenly announced that Charles had no right to the family name anyway as his father was illegitimate and had only adopted that name. She also let slip that she was illegitimate and her father was a traveller passing by who stayed with her mother (Charles's grandmother) for the next sixteen years before remembering that he had a wife at home in Norfolk. He came from a bricklayer's family. Well, so much for all the airs and graces and calling me rubbish, while my family had an eleventh-century and coat of arms which was a lynx. I must admit I enjoyed passing on this information.

As always, I wanted Charles and my mother to be proud of me, and I strived to make the best of everything. I became a deputy head teacher and enjoyed the change. Then I relentlessly applied for the post of head teacher. I wanted to be someone to be proud of and not just another foreigner. At last, the day came, and I was appointed to the post at a large infant school in Edgware. Oh! I was so proud! I had made it. Surely Charles would now be proud of me, but alas, I think he resented my success. My mother too exclaimed that I was just a caretaker, but my sister in Germany, was a fantastic teacher, and her two boys were something to be proud of, as they were so clever and handsome. I could not hold a candle to her.

Well, I was proud of myself and pleased with my success, having reached one of my goals I was determined to make my professional life a success, even if I could not help cowering before my husband's wrath or stop being a doormat at home. I would try to succeed.

I involved Charles in various ways, but sadly he became 'difficult' at all times. Why could I not win when I loved him so much? Oh, I tried so hard to be thought of as English and do everything correctly. At the same time, there was the pull of my German heritage. Would I ever be free to be just me? I kept asking myself: *Who am I? What am I?*

As the children grew up and did not need me any more, my school life became the most exciting part in my life. I could hardly wait for each day to start and planned many innovative ideas. I wanted to run my school like no other, and my staff and parents backed me whole-heartedly.

I introduced family grouping and parent committees and created a library and a loan service of books as well as a toy-lending library. I fought and won to get a Suzuki teacher to teach violin to the children who wanted to learn, while I taught recorder so that we could have a little orchestra in the school, supplemented with percussion. I had a great bunch of teachers, without whom I could have achieved nothing.

I was allowed to paint the classrooms at the weekends and was given money to carpet the school throughout. We also put up a great many display boards to stimulate the children and then show off their work.

Science corners, cookery rooms, and even a shower room were added to make this a caring environment.

My policy was to value each child, each nationality, and each religion, so I put on various festivals, depicting the important religious festivals in each country, and as we had thirty-eight different languages in the school, this became an exciting event, with parents, priests, and rabbis contributing and helping me make a success of each event. I also took the staff to various places of worship so they could learn and understand the basic principles and know what the parents believed in. They were fun outings, and we all learnt a great deal.

We held Guy Fawkes parties, after receiving special permission and alerting the fire brigade and the police in case of trouble. No one had ever done this before, and it became a great annual event with 500 people attending on the given night.

The Christmas Fair was a special event. We made a Father Christmas Grotto, through which the children had to find their way in order to see Father Christmas, talk to him, and receive a present. It was magic. Parents helped and contributed to the bazaar, and we raised at least two thousand pounds for the school fund. How I loved counting the money!

At other times, the BBC came to film, and we enjoyed being on television—great excitement. Not that we were lacking in academic standard, by any means. We came up as one of the top infant schools in the UK, after the Ofsted inspections. I am forever grateful to my wonderful and dedicated staff, who worked so hard and supported me in every way. I really love my happy time at school.

I wanted to be *me*, but still felt somewhat of a foreigner and belied my background.

The boys, who were all excellent swimmers, started to teach swimming to other children under the guidance of a school for swimming and earned extra money. Brian, too, started teaching and lied about his age so that he could take the necessary lifesaving certificates. I told him he must not lie but could smudge his date of birth so it became illegible. He also took up bodybuilding and physical training as an instructor.

All the boys learnt to drive a car, and Charles took them around local car parks for their lesson. I then went out driving with them, often with my heart in my mouth as they loved to show off for me. However, they all passed their driving test and became excellent drivers.

Surprise parties for Charles were planned every year.

To celebrate the New Year, we would have nearly eighty people come to our house, and I would provide the buffet meal. I loved all the preparation and to then see everyone enjoy themselves. The children too would join in, as they grew older. At midnight, we would join hands and sing 'Auld Lang Syne', and Charles would enjoy kissing everyone, but sadly would forget me. I always went upstairs to kiss the youngest members of the family and even wish the dogs a happy new year.

Charles was the perfect host and really enjoyed the parties, plying everyone lavishly with food and drink. By 3.00 a.m., all departed, and I started to clear up as I hated the small of stale smoke and alcohol the next morning. Although I was not very good at party talk, I loved the preparations and serving all our friends. We loved our parties, and they became famous within our circle of friends.

As the boys completed their A levels and applied for university, I again fought hard to get them to the best places and wrote numerous letter for them. Before they continued their further education I suggested travel for them. At that time, a gap year was not talked about but I wanted them to see something of the world before settling down to further study and then job hunting. Richard and Tim travelled widely around India and Africa. Stephanie too, when the time came, took a journey to explore India.

Brian decided that he was not like his brothers and just walked out of his A level exams. He told me he wanted to be like Richard Branson and become a millionaire by the time he was thirty. He did not need further studies.

Proudly we visited the universities, whenever they had an Open day and were really proud when attending their graduation day. Even my mother came over from Germany to celebrate the occasions.

The time had come yet again for Charles to lock horns, this time with Brian. He shouted at him to do as he said or get out. Brian, being a chip off the old block just said nothing and departed for the USA, which he had planned as his year off. The two of them hardly spoke to each other for the next twenty years. I could see that Brian was very hurt and could see the pain in Charles's eyes, but there was nothing I could do. So I decided to travel to Los Angeles to visit Brian and see for myself how he was getting on. I was very excited and delighted when he met me at the airport. I stayed with him at his digs, and we had a great time together. He introduced me to all his friends and in a borrowed a car went sightseeing. We saw all the old Spanish Los Angeles, had meals out, and enjoyed being together. On the way home, the car's brakes failed and we narrowly escaped a crash as we sailed down a steep hill at an important intersection. A few days after the brakes were fixed, we explored the Palisades, when the engine caught fire. I decided there and then that Brian must have his own transport, and as he had talked about getting a motorbike, I went out and bought him a second hand bike. From then on I had to ride pillion behind Brian, which was quite hairy at times. For a change, Brian took me cycling on the beach from Sunset Boulevard to Santa Monica. As I had not ridden a bike for a long time, we rented a tandem bike and I had to sit in front, while he would steady the bike from behind—or so I thought. I wondered why the going was so hard, when I realized that Brian was sitting behind me with his feet up, letting me do all the work. We could not stop laughing.

For Brian's twenty-first birthday, I planned a surprise visit to the States again, in order to celebrate his birthday. Charles came with me, and Brian just could not get over his surprise, saying, 'Dad, my Dad' over and over again. Sadly, this state did not last long, and yet again Charles did not speak to him and I ended up in floods of tears. Never would I go with him to visit Brian again, although I regularly visited by myself every two years.

The girls grew up fast and the day came that Charles resented Cindy's presence, saying that she drove Brian away and he no longer wanted her in his house. I thought that perhaps the time had come that Cindy lived with a black family, to get to know her roots. We lost touch with her for a few years.

My good guardian angel or good fairy seemed to have deserted me, and I realized that something had gone seriously wrong in my married life. I still loved Charles passionately but could get little or no response from him. I tried to get him to make love to me, but it became more and more difficult. Some years before, he had stopped altogether. I tried hard to seduce him and only managed it seldom. I always felt that the whole world should be able to see that I had been made love to. I felt reborn. Sadly those occasions became less and less frequent, and I just could not understand it at all. A grope in the dark, the nighty would be pushed up, and then two minutes later, wham, bam and without as much as a thank you ma'am, he would be asleep, while I wondered what it was all about. What was wrong with me? All my friends talked about twice weekly sessions, and I kept quiet. Why could I not be a siren in the bedroom? How could I learn when there was no one to ask? Soon everything to do with sex stopped, but at least I had my cuddles. He appeared loving and caring and as always thanked me profusely after each meal I cooked. However, I still longed for him to love me and dreamt that one day he would want me again as a woman.

I know that a lot of women must feel as I do and perhaps have the same experiences. Do they know what to do? To have failed as a sexual partner is not something one wants to talk about or even share with ones friends. I really feel for those ladies. Why has fate shortchanged me? What should I have done better?

I would often recall a dream that I had before I got married, when I questioned how I would know whether the man I planned to marry was right for me. I was walking with a tall dark, cloaked figure, who put his arms about me and I felt so loved and safe at that moment. He was my guardian angel he said, and when I was with a man and had that wonderful feeling again, I would know that he was right for me. And thus it always was when I was in Charles's arms. I had felt so safe, warm, and loved. Please let that continue.

The children having left home for university, we moved house and found a lovely house in Whetstone, with four bedrooms. I was so sad to leave our last house and felt as if all I had ever worked for and hoped for was coming apart. I did not want to leave our lovely home where we had been so happy. Charles even named the house 'Bounty', after all our blessings as well as seeing himself as the renegade captain Blyth of the ship bearing that name. It was a suitable name as we felt to be very lucky and sailed through life on both stormy and gentle, sun-lit days.

I continued to plan all different kind of surprises for Charles as birthday or anniversary treats. There were visits to theatres, special restaurants, and presents galore. I even planned a surprise trip to Paris for Charles and Stephanie. I told them to be ready for a weekend trip and in the last minute asked for their passports. They had no idea of where they were going. We arrived at the airport and joined Air India checking-in counter. I then presented them both with a little guidebook about Paris. The hotel was booked by phone and flowers for Stephanie and champagne for Charles awaited them. It was a good trip but at times spoilt by Charles's emotional bullying.

The new house was soon decorated through Charles's magic touch and felt like home. A house-warming party and even the christening of a cement elephant as a fountain in our garden was celebrated with all our friends. One of them dressed up as the Queen to cut the ribbons.

The animals had left some time before, as I took them to school to have a little farm for the children to enjoy. I had come to lead a double life. I loved school and could be myself, planning and putting into practice all I believed. We put on concerts and plays; were even invited to take the whole school to perform our Christmas play at the National Theatre, which was amazing and a great success.

I started a nursery at the school and started a drama class that continued with the same children for the next ten years, even when they had left school. A young music student, Adam, and I joined forces and founded 'The Kids from Barnet Musical Theatre' and the children between the ages four and sixteen from various schools in Barnet joined our venture. We performed on TV, radio, and at the National Theatre. Adam wrote the music, and I the lyrics, and we enjoyed a good reputation and raised money for the Royal Free Hospital and for Save the Children Fund.

Adam became a great friend, and as he was only a few years older than my eldest son, we welcomed him into our family. He taught the children music, percussion and came on holiday with us. We had a great working relationship with never a cross word. The drama group went from strength to strength and we soon had eighty children who met regularly in a church hall in Finchley, London. We were both so enthusiastic and loved every moment. Sadly, when Adam died, I discontinued the group. I still hear from the children, some twenty years later.

I bought a Great Dane and took the dog to school, so that no child would be afraid of dogs as I had been. My little farm of pony, goats, and chickens became a feature at school and the children would take it in turn to care for them and collect eggs with which to bake, as part of their lessons. When I had an inspection, this initiative was greatly praised.

I had made quite a name for myself in educational circles so that I was headhunted to become an inspector and advisor at the education office. Part of my job was a PR representative for the borough and to travel around the country recruiting new staff to join Barnet's teaching force. We designed exhibition materials, and I wrote booklets for students who wanted to become teachers. I really enjoyed travelling around the country.

As all through my life, my flying dreams continued, and by then, I was very proficient and could take off from the ground rather than having to jump out of windows. I loved the feeling of freedom as I flew higher and higher under a star-lit sky or soared high above trees and houses on sunny days. I also visited many places that only existed in my dreams. Some of those I would revisit on several occasions.

Sometime during these years, William and then Charles's mother died. We had the funeral and had to clear up her house. Charles never even cried, and I wondered whether he even grieved. My mother was visiting at the time, and I was glad of her company, because I was afraid to be left alone in Nanny's house, thinking her ghost would come out to confront and haunt me. I was most relieved when all the clearing up was finished and we could leave that house forever.

My sister had married some years before, but I, being pregnant and about to deliver, could not attend the wedding, which was a grand affair and nothing like mine. My mother had organized everything, and most of my family and her friends attended. When I went to visit her, I tried on her bridal gown and felt absolutely fantastic as a bride. Charles was not there, and I wished he could have seen me as a radiant bride. So I just took some photos of what could have been.

After my sister was married with children of her own, as my mother was on her own, so I visited her every year or so. Charles was not happy about my going, and I had to start making overtures three months before I wanted to travel so he would give me permission. As she became unwell my visits were not so much a holiday as just being with her. She was always pleased to see me. Over the years, I got proficient at finding cheap airfares, travelling with various airlines that have long ago gone out of existence. I also became very good at smuggling in pounds of tea and coffee, trying to cover the naughty goods with sanitary towels, thinking that the custom officials would be too embarrassed to search further.

I usually stayed for a long weekend and made sure everything at home was left prepared for Charles. However, he would usually go to one of his girlfriends and then telephone me three times a day. When he did accompany me, he usually became very impatient when sitting around the house, watching television, and hearing my mother and me remember old times, sing together, or recite poems that I learnt as a child. I was amazed at how many German songs I knew from the past. They seemed part of me and poured forth at the slightest invitation. Where and when did I learn them and how come I still remember them now, so many years later? It is strange to realize how many things become part of one's personality without being aware of it.

Again and again I ask myself, am I German or British.

Before my mother became ill, she would travel a great deal, all over the world. One day, she invited me to come with her to North America—New England and Canada. She would pay for everything. I begged Charles for a long time to let me go, and eventually he agreed. It was a lovely trip, and I really enjoyed being with my mother, who I adored and looked up to so much, even if she did not appreciate me. Therefore, I was really grateful to be given the chance to enjoy being with her and sharing her love of travel. I took with me a little tape recorder and recorded everything I saw, describing it at length. I also recorded sounds such as the The Liberty Bell in Pennsylvania, the sound of the water cascading down Niagara Falls, as well as describing many other interesting places and sent them home so that Charles could share my discoveries with me. Years later, I found all the un-opened letters. He never read any of them.

On my return, he seemed sad that he had not travelled there, so I planned a trip for him to follow in my footsteps, and he eagerly set off for the States.

A few years later, I got his permission to visit Russia and Japan with my mother. We went on the Siberian Express across Russia, having flown into Moscow, accompanied by Russian MIG jets. We loved being in Moscow as it reminded up of somewhat of living in Czechoslovakia. We tried our poorly remembered Czech and learnt some more Russian. We loved deciphering the Russian words that we saw, such as street names and names on the underground stops, although the Russian script was different from ours. From there we visited Bratsk, the largest and deepest fresh water lake in Europe and from there boarded the train in Irkutsk. Siberia was great, and the journey from Vladivostok to Japan by boat was a real treat.

I loved Japan, and found Tokyo really interesting. It was quite difficult to travel by underground as all the names were written in Japanese script, which we could not read. I had written to our Japanese friends, former students, that I was coming, so they came to visit us at the hotel and took us out to dinner. It was lovely to see them again, and I would have liked to meet their families, but they said it was not their custom to entertain at home and thus they treated us to delicious Japanese food in various eating places. We had a really interesting time, which all too soon came to an end. This time I kept a diary and recorded all the events every day for Charles to share. Those, too, remained unread.

The years passed, and soon we were about to celebrate out twenty-fifth wedding anniversary. Charles usually forgot these occasions and would rush to Tesco to buy bath foam and many little things that he could find to give as a present from all the animals as well as from himself. A couple of times he really excelled himself by buying me a TV recorder that I had longed for, and another time I came home on my birthday to find a brand new car waiting for me on the drive. I was overcome and burst into tears.

Mainly celebrations would be up me to plan. I loved thinking out special surprises for him and would gladly pluck the stars out of the skies if that was what he wanted. Once, thinking that he wanted to learn sailing, I bought him a Mirror dingy and found a sailing club for him to join. This was a very special boat, as it was only the fifteenth produced and was a collector's piece. He was delighted and pleased to join the club but sadly soon lost interest and the boat was left to rot outside our garage.

For our twenty-fifth anniversary, unknown to him, I booked a local hall and wrote to all our friends inviting them to a party. As they all, more or less, belonged to the theatre club and loved Music Hall, I asked them to come dressed up in Victorian costume and then sing one of their favourite songs. Thus, I had instant entertainment laid on. I cleaned and decorated the hall and prepared a full buffet supper. Charles did query all my cooking, but I said I was helping my friend Margaret for a function that she had to prepare for. The boys helped by asking their dad to go swimming and my friend Adam requested Charles's company that evening to help him at a concert, telling him to dress smartly. I had written instructions of how to get to the hall and swore everyone to secrecy so that Charles would be surprised. At last the day came. My mother happened to be here on a visit so we both went to the theatre club to borrow some costumes. I dressed in a beautiful Victorian dress, head decorations, and jewellery and felt like a million dollars.

Over eighty people turned up, regally dressed for the occasion, and when Charles arrived at the hall, supposedly to pick up some loud speakers, he was stunned. We had a fantastic evening. Richard and Tim came down from the university and prepared an act, and Stephanie, who was in India at the time, had recorded a special song for him. The whole event was video filmed as a special memento for Charles and presented to him at a later date with a letter from me thanking him for the wonderful twenty-five years and expressing how much I loved him, a love that continued to grow year by year and would do so till death do us part. I looked forward to the next twenty-five years, travel, and then, hopefully, grandchildren to share our old age.

Charles was in his element and enjoyed every moment of the evening, giving a witty speech but forgetting all about me until the audience reminded him that as it was our anniversary I should share the moment with him. All went off well and would be remembered for a long time.

I had continued enjoying my success at work, but sadly Charles became very dissatisfied with his own job. He was not really interested in VAT and office work and therefore not surprisingly did not manage to get further promotion. Thus, I encouraged him to take early retirement from the civil service and freeze his pension money. I continued to take in students to help boost the income. Next, I tried to get him to decide what he wanted to do. He thought he wanted to teach but then declined. Feeling jealous of the children's freedom to travel, he thought he wanted to go to India and discover places his father had lived in when a young man, before marrying his mother. We prepared everything and I threw a farewell party for him to give him a great send off. Leaving the following day, he followed in his father's footsteps, and we planned that as soon as I started my holiday, I would follow on and meet him in Delhi. It was a lovely reunion, as I had missed him so. Together we travelled around the golden triangle, Varanesi and Rajestan, where we went on a camel safari—Ouch!—I thought I would never be able to walk properly again. We had a fantastic time and returned full of plans for future travel.

Another time, we met Richard and his girlfriend (now his wife) in Kenya and joined them on safari in the Masai Mara. It was a great holiday, and we met many interesting people and visited various tribes in their villages. Richard was a great guide and had planned the whole trip for us. He had booked a four-wheel drive car. We met in Nairobi and then explored the Masai Mara, finding our own way around. I was really frightened when we lost the track and found ourselves amongst a pride of lions. I was happy that they were not interested in us. Next, we stalled the car amongst a herd of elephants, and the horn got stuck so that it hooted loudly. The elephants got restless and came towards us, ears flapping. Just in time we managed to get away. By then darkness had fallen, and it was forbidden to drive around the reservation in the dark. What could we do? We had lost our way and had to persevere. Luckily, we met a ranger, who told us we were on the correct track. We drove through the darkness and saw many threatening outlines of elephants, water buffalo, or some other animals like that, before we saw the twinkling lights of a compound ahead. We had a luxury apartment with all modern amenities. We enjoyed all the comforts that were on offer and soon forgot the stress of the past few hours. Richard and Judy chose to camp out and had their very own Masai warrior guarding them outside their tent, in case of being attacked by lions or hyenas. They were young and adventurous, but I preferred nestling down with Charles in a comfy bed. Must be getting old!

Next, we headed north towards Lake Turkhana, but not before Judy bought a Masai blanket off a young warrior and enjoyed wearing it and smelling it.

We stayed by Lake Naivasha and Lake Baikal, where hippos visited us as we were sitting outside, eating our supper when Richard said, 'Mother, don't turn round, but there is a hippo behind you.' I thought he was joking, but the animal, as large as the side of a house, stood there and looked at me, before continuing on his walk, while I sat frozen to my seat.

The journey to Lake Turkhana was very memorable. There was no road or path. We drove through the bush and met only some shepherds and a Masai who wanted a lift. He sat next to me in the car, beautifully made up as a young warrior, and wearing his blanket as well as Marks and Spencer's socks and a wristwatch! He spoke no English so we conversed in mime. Suddenly he cried 'Stop!' in the middle of nowhere and pointed to where he lived and invited us for a cup of tea. We got out of the car and followed him. Just beyond our immediate sight, we saw a group of huts and people running out to greet us. The boy's older brother was a teacher and spoke English, so he showed us round. We sat in a mud hut, sipping tea (I did not question how or where the water came from and how it was made). The hut was decorated with cornflake boxes and pictures out of magazines. They were lovely people and gave us instructions of how to continue our journey. We thanked them and took photos to send to them from the UK. I do not know whether they ever received them.

The next part of our journey was across a very rough terrain of volcanic rocks. It was a huge area, and one could think that we had landed on the moon. There was nothing to be seen except lava rocks. The car we borrowed rocked its way across. I lived on my nerves again, as I worried that the car, being slung so low, could easily hit the rocks and damage the suspension, the sump, and engine parts. How could we get help, when no one in the world knew where we were and we had seen no-one pass us along the way? We also heard reports of shooting and raiding from tribes across the borders of Somalia. *Help!* However, the fates were kind and protected us, and we safely made our way across the rocks and reached the lake in one piece.

Lake Turkhana was enormous and inhabited by fisher folk, who lived in what I can only describe as turned up laundry baskets. Everything smelled of fish. Children came running out of nowhere, and we gave them biro pens, which we had been told would be very welcome. Waving them goodbye, we made our way to a visitor's compound, also in the middle of nowhere. This was paradise lost and found—a complete sanctuary and haven of luxury. There was a swimming pool fed by a hot spring, and all the little huts had hot running water. The food was the very best that any first-class restaurant anywhere in the world could offer. The ingredients were flown in fresh daily from Nairobi by a special plane, which was resting on the airstrip outside. We had a wonderful stay there and were very sorry to leave.

We made our way back, driving down the other side of the country on fairly good roads, passing Mount Kenya, and drove to Mombassa. We stayed in an old, colonial hotel that had seen much better days, and was very dilapidated, as indeed was everything else we saw. Thus we made our way to a little village, where we stayed in huts, by the sea's edge and built specially for tourists. We relaxed in the beautifully warm sea, sunbathed, and enjoyed life. Charles decided to stay on and take a paddy course in diving while we drove back to Nairobi. I had a plane to catch back to the UK and start work again, and Charles said he would come back at a later date.

I returned home tired but happy, while Richard and Judy continued their trip around Africa.

When Tim was travelling around Mexico, we planned to meet for Christmas in Mexico City and then continue travelling together. We explored much of the country, the numerous pyramids and temples, and stayed in some delightful towns in the mountains. We even slept on a nudist beach in hammocks, somewhere south of Acapulco. I must say that after my first embarrassment of seeing all those naked men, I became fascinated with God's design of the different genitalia that I saw. *Wow!*

On the beach were stands where the locals cooked delicious Mexican food for us. The most amazing and incongruous thing for me was a proper European china toilet that was plumbed in on the beach. It had a scruffy curtain around it to give privacy to the users. I shall not forget that sight in a hurry. I brought with me presents and of course a small plastic Christmas tree that we decorated. 'Silent night, holy night' on the beach, under a bright star-lit night was quite something.

During the day we lazed on the sand, swam, or practiced tai-chi. Why does time always seem to fly by when one is really enjoying oneself?

I had to get back to England but as Charles was not working, he continued travelling to Guatemala and other neighbouring places on his own, while Tim and his friends went on their way. I was so pleased when Charles returned home, safe and sound.

The time had come for Charles to find some sort of employment that would satisfy him. As he always enjoyed home decorating and excelled at it, he decided to start up a business that he called 'In the Nick of Time'. Having found out about special awards and training available for people that wanted to start their own firm, Charles duly enrolled. However, he would not take any advice and advertise himself, so all the work that he found was with friends, whom he felt he could not charge. Having met a friend of mine from the Education Office who was doing the same sort of work, I encouraged them to join forces, but Charles fell out with him and that was that.

A neighbour of ours who we befriended wanted to start a shop with design furniture and Charles became excited with the idea, so he put up the money and they opened a special shop selling only the most wonderful designs in furnishings. I was very proud of him and we all tried to help where we could.

Following in his mother's footsteps, Charles always fell out with friends after a certain time, and thus it came to pass that this venture was short lived, and Charles lost a great deal of money and good friends.

Working on his own, he then bought a derelict house and redeveloped it, before selling it again. Next, he bought an old house and split it into two flats and modernized everything before selling them both. He was so clever and could adapt and turn his hand to anything. Any ideas coming from me were frowned upon, so that I found it difficult to help him. I did not want to be pushy or bossy.

Time passed.

I decided to study for my master's degree, but Charles made this very difficult for me, by asking his special friends round for meals whenever I had a deadline for an assignment. First, it was Vivienne, with whom he always spent a great deal of time, saying he had to help her as she was all on her own and had very few friends. After eight years, she suddenly disappeared from the scene, and we could not find out why. Next came X, Y, and Z—always women on their own, with or without children, who needed Charles's special help. I was proud of him that he wanted to help others less lucky than us. We always seemed to pick up the lonely or helpless and even took them on holiday with us. It was a way of paying back for our happiness and good luck.

Suddenly, out of the blue, fate stepped in. Our happiness seemed to dim considerably. Charles became very moody and bullying in every way. He would not speak to me weeks on end without giving any reason. I felt very helpless but never stopped loving him. I tried planning another wedding anniversary by going to a secluded country hotel with him. I bought special underwear, nightdress, and smart clothes to celebrate in. It was a terrible mistake. Instead of bringing us together, it made an even greater rift. Charles took no notice, deciding to watch football all weekend while I sobbed myself to sleep, heartbroken.

Another Time, Another Place

As my sixtieth birthday approached, I planned a special trip for us. I had done the same on my fiftieth, and we had travelled to Jerusalem and the Holy Land. The boys sent a special telegram as if from the Queen. We had a superb time. Thus, I planned a trip down the Nile in Egypt to mark my sixtieth birthday. However, for one reason or another, Charles had stopped talking to me, and I had no idea why. He had done this frequently in the past but eventually recovered from his mood and stopped punishing me in this way. This time, weeks went past, and he still did not speak to me. I was at my wits end, not knowing what to do. I invited friends round, included him in everything I did, but all was to no avail.

In desperation, I suggested to him that as he was not speaking with me, should I go alone on my holiday, for it appeared to me that he wanted nothing to do with me. Instead of shocking him out of his misery, for we never did anything alone and were always together, he just said to do as I wished. He had no desire to travel down the Nile. I completed all arrangements for my travel alone.

The night before my journey, I came home and to my great surprise found that a birthday party had been arranged for me and all our children and friends were there waiting for me to celebrate my sixtieth birthday. I just stood in amazement as Charles had never before arranged a party for me. Oh, surely that is a sign that he did love me after all and was sorry. I was just overcome with joy and the evening passed as if in a dream. Suddenly, I came to realize that Charles had organized nothing, and it was my daughter Stephanie, who had invited and planned everything from Edinburgh, where she was at university. It was all her doing.

The next day, Charles took me to the airport. I clung to him, weeping, saying that I did not want to go on my own. I loved him desperately and needed him. Without him I was just nothing as he gave me all the confidence to do, plan, and carry out tasks in my life. I would never have been a head teacher or arts administrator without him backing me up. How could I now travel without him by my side, especially on this special occasion?

In tears I bade him bye and left for my journey.

It was a wonderful trip on the old King Farouk's Nile paddle steamer, with only twelve cabins. I felt so lost, although everyone on the party was very nice. The crew, knowing it was my birthday, had baked a special cake and all present celebrated by birthday. I missed Charles every moment of the trip and so badly wanted to share all the adventure with me.

I could hardly wait meeting Charles at the airport on my return, but sadly nothing had changed and all was silence.

Sometime later that year I sat in the sitting room weeping and told Nick that I had just heard from my sister that my mother was critically ill, having had a heart attack and a stroke, She had already had a triple bypass and was not expected to make the night. I was desolate. As if that was not bad enough, I had just heard from the education office that educational funds from central government had run out and as there now was no job for me. I would have to retire. I had just finished a stint at a primary school where I was asked to troubleshoot and guide the school into good practice. There was no party or celebration for my retirement—not even after thirty-five years of service. Now nobody wanted me.

'Well, so what? I don't want you either!' was all the comfort I received after forty years of marriage. What had I done wrong, except perhaps love Charles too much?

On Brian's following birthday, I set out once more to visit him in Los Angeles. As always on my visits, we had a great time, and I was made welcome by all his friends. I dreaded my return home, as I guessed that Charles would give me a hard time. And oh boy, he did. Firstly he had locked me out of the house on my return so that I could not get in after my long journey. It was snowing and I was dressed for warm weather. I left my suitcase with neighbours and went to a cafe to keep warm.

Later, I tried again to go home. Eventually Charles returned, having been with our friend George and not caring about coming home to meet me. When he did come, he sat in the kitchen, drinking steadily until he was well and truly in his cups. He shouted and swore at me all the time, banging his fist on the table and eventually told me to get out.

'You and your son, just get out of my life!'

I asked him if he really meant it and then said that if that was his wish, I would go. At this point Charles withdrew up to bed, urging me to get out of his life.

I was devastated, frightened and just did not know what to do. When Charles was angry, I was always frightened—not that he ever lifted a finger against me—but words were crueller. I took my overnight bag, as I had not even unpacked, took my dog, the Great Dane Penny, and left the house in my car with no idea where to go.

So there I was, on a cold and snowing February night, huddled in my car with the dog spending the night in a car park. I have no words to describe my misery.

Chapter 19

The night was freezing and wet, but somehow Penny and I survived the car park. I phoned my friend Margaret, who by then was living in Brighton and sobbed my woes down the telephone. She invited me for the weekend. Next I went to see George, Charles's closest friend who was a father figure to him. I thought he would be able to make Charles see sense. He did not want to interfere.

Next, I went to see Hilde and Sophie, my former guardians from the hostel days with whom I had faithfully stayed in touch and had visited them regularly. I told them what had happened, but they didn't want to know. Would no one help me?

My mother had died. How I wish I could have talked to her, I missed her terribly, as over the past few years I had phoned her every day. Realizing now she was dead, I would no longer be pulled two ways. I could be truly British—*too late!*

Having nowhere to go, I booked myself in to a B and B, frequented by long-distance lorry drivers, where my dog and I could stay. I was very nervous staying there but the dog cuddled close and looked after me by growling as soon as anyone came near the room. I was too frightened to find a toilet, so standing on a chair and using my balance I used the sink. It wasn't funny. The next morning I went to Brighton to see Margaret.

Returning to London, I haunted all the estate agents for a room to rent. At last I was lucky and found a place with a garden that would take both me and my dog. I also found a part-time job as a lecturer in education, so could pay my rent.

I wrote long letters to Charles, telling him where I was and what I was doing. I never received an answer.

Needing clothes, I asked a friend to come to our house with me and stand guard, in case Charles came home. Although I armed myself with Valium tablets, I was terrified. The only other item I took was the television, so that I could take comfort by escaping reality.

Blaming myself for everything, I wrote to Charles with a mea culpa.

The friends I still saw said I was lucky to be out of reach of all the emotional bullying and should get on with my life. Oh, it was so easy for everyone else to make these comments, but I was slowly sinking deeper and deeper into misery.

When my lump sum and pension came through, I looked for a house, thinking that when Charles came back we could rent it out and have an extra income. I was lucky to find house overlooking a park. The scenery from the bedroom window was of a manor house with cows grazing in the fields. Where in London could one be so fortunate?

I bought an English Setter puppy, Molly, so that Penny, who had died when only three, would never be alone. Often, I would sob over Molly, when I was sad and miserable.

I felt proud of myself to have purchased the house all by myself, going through all the legal requirements, land registration, and other formalities. I decorated the house, found furniture, and created a garden.

Charles and I met monthly. I was in seventh heaven as I hoped in this way things would improve. However, he never discussed what had gone wrong and just kept saying that one day soon we would be together. I lived in hope. I spoke to the trees and the bubbling brooks all the words that I wanted Charles to hear. I must have seemed a crazy old woman seen ambling along and muttering to myself.

One day, Stephanie came to me to inform me that Charles had a girlfriend and that I was living in cuckoo land hoping for him to return. I took twenty tablets of Valium and rushed round to the house to question him.

Yes, he had a girlfriend, but only for sex. If all he wanted was sex, why did he not sleep with me for the past thirty years?

A year passed. I became obsessed, thinking of that woman. I would get up in the night, and in pyjamas would drive past the house.

As I had every right to be in the house, I returned home letting Stephanie and her partner live in my new house. There is no fury like a woman scorned, and I was on the warpath, which gave me courage. For the next three years I lived in the house, like a bedsit, cooking in a microwave in the bathroom. Little bit, by little bit I started cooking downstairs and invited Charles to share the food. I would prepare his dinner and leave the room so as not to crowd him. I offered to do his washing. Perhaps I could find my way back to him through home comforts. He could keep his whores and go out with them every night. Easier said than done.

Oh, you stupid, old woman Daisy.

I often tried to plead with Charles to live with me once again. He could sleep with whom he wanted. Soon we would have grandchildren and could enjoy them. I cried, I stormed, I knelt before him. I made a fool of myself and debased myself completely. I hated myself for being so weak and not letting go, but I just did not care. Poor Charles, it must have been terribly embarrassing for him and all he could say was, 'We will. We shall. Let's see.'

So I waited.

My job had become to an end at the college, but before leaving I persuaded someone to give Charles a job at the college teaching English to overseas students, something he had always wanted.

One day, I found out that for years Charles, had been womanizing and chasing after everyone in a skirt. Impossible—Charles was loyal to me. Asking around, I found out that Charles had affairs all over the place and an eight-year relationship with a family friend. My head was reeling, and I phoned her immediately. She answered in the affirmative saying that she had slept with Charles for over eight years but was not proud of it at all.

Oh, I just wanted the floor to swallow me. My husband had slept around for years, and I never knew. How, when, and why? How many other women? How could I be so stupid? I was shaking and hurting so much that I picked up a carving knife to cut my arm and stop the hurt within me. I wanted to cut the thought of all these women out of my mind. The knife was too blunt and would not cut, so I sharpened it and tried again. I only managed three small cuts as the skin kept moving, and I could not get a bigger cut. Once bleeding, I felt better, but was inconsolable.

Some weeks later, Charles and I were having supper together when I questioned him about his unfaithfulness. He said that it had nothing to do with me. I tried to reason with him, saying that I was his wife and had been so for the past thirty years or more. I was cutting up French bread at the time and brandishing the knife while I was talking. I retorted that his words hurt me more than if I cut myself. At this point, the breadknife fell and lacerated my arm right to the bone.

This time it was a real accident. Blood spurted out everywhere, but Charles jumped up swearing at me and left the room and the house. I called out for help, needing go the hospital. First, I put my dog on a lead as I did not want her to taste human blood by lapping it up—what a bizarre thought!

Stephanie drove round to fetch me. I walked to meet her, thinking the fresh air would stop me from passing out. I had covered the arm with towels to staunch the bleeding and not frighten my daughter. Hospital visits, more stitching, and finally operations followed and I still bear all the scars. I even had to apologize to Charles for causing a problem.

Still obsessed with him, I cried myself to sleep every night. I wanted to hurt myself more and more and even went to the hospital asking for psychological help. None was available. I became desperate and went to see various counsellors, private psychotherapists, faith healers, attended re-birthing sessions, saw people who looked into the future and the past—in fact anyone who thought they could help me. I studied my horoscopes and attended tarot card readings. I even went to the Spiritualist Society of Great Britain to seek help but all to no avail. Charlatans—the lot of them. How stupid can I be?

I tried to take stock of myself. I was born unwanted and pushed from pillar to post when all I wanted was to belong and be loved by people, especially my husband. I always tried to better myself—at what expense I wondered. I loved to look after people and to help them. Was I too pushy and suffocating? Had I, in my seeking for love and approval, made myself into a martyr and underdog? Who could help me now?

I tried to escape by travelling to Cyprus and find work there but became very ill with ulcerated colitis and had to return to the UK for major surgery.

I wanted my mother. With whom could I could I discuss this? Well, I guess we are born on our own and die on our own.

I told the consultants to do their worst. Jokingly said to the big man (consultant to the Queen, no less) that while he was operating, could he please give me a face-lift and tummy tuck at the same time. He was not amused.

'Madam,' he said, 'I do not do things like that!'

The others in his party hid their smiles and later came to me and said, that as the surgeon only dealt with bottoms and the nether region, would I really like to have a face like an old bottom? We all laughed. I consented to the operation but was terrified. What would be the outcome? I was told that I would have a stoma bag for the rest of my life but had no idea what it would be like. Would there be pipes and clamps attached to my stomach? Would I need to carry a little container or handbag to hold all the equipment? Well, let it be my girl. See what happens.

If I had to die, please let it be while I was unconscious, as I did not want to wake up and find out that I was dead.

At that point in time, while the surgeon was sharpening his scalpels, the phone rang. It was Charles demanding a divorce and telling me that I must sell the house. I had thought nothing more or worse could happen to me to me now.

What timing!

It was a cold, wet day and the wind was howling around the building, just as it had the day I was born. There was no joy and cries of delight and no glittering future ahead. There was just emptiness, loneliness, and heartache. I was so ashamed of myself. I buried my head under the hospital sheets and wanted to find a hole to hide in or the earth to swallow me up. I had enough.

Let all the rest be silence.

Postscript

I came to in my hospital bed and found that I had not shuffled off this mortal coil. I was wired up and attached to numerous tubes, bags and apparatus.

Interesting. Now what?

Lawyers.

Selling my home.

A divorce I don't want.

I cried copious tears. I raved, ranted and pleaded but all in vain.

I may not be a beautiful woman—not slim and sexy—but to hell with all that. I am fairly intelligent, creative, kind and generous, helpful, understanding, musical and artistic. I am full of energy, fun, with a zest for living. So my girl, make the most of life and count your blessings.

Perhaps my father named me aptly. I am the little weed that everyone trampled on, but I jump up every time and with my little golden center—my heart of gold—survive and give others pleasure.

I may be old but there is still life in the old dog (or should I say bitch?) yet. I have adopted a motto—*Feel the fear but do it anyway.*

Thinking of my wonderful and free childhood in Bavaria, my successes as a professional, my children whom, I have seen through university, my remaining friends, I see that I am blessed and a very rich person.

Why should I be afraid? One only dies once. Ah, that however is still my fear. I desperately want to live and achieve something more in life.

I find that I am still afraid of ghosts even though my mother and I made a pact, that whosoever dies first, would come and tell the other one what it was like and allay the fear. Until now she has not appeared and I am still waiting.

My little inner girl is never far from the surface. She asks me questions and prompts me into action. Oh, I am so unsure of so many things and blunder on regardless, acting as if I am full of confidence. Well they do say you can fool most of the people most of the time—so I try.

My children are now married and have children of their own. I went to their weddings, armed with drugs because of Charles' presence, who of course, played the part of a loving husband to the public gallery.

On the way back from one particular set of nuptials, I fell asleep whilst driving on the motorway and my car started to weave in and out between great big juggernaut lorries. How I did not get killed I shall never know.

Someone up there above the clouds must have been watching over me, and wanted me to live.

With seven grandchildren I am so happy and proud. How can I feel sad and lonely?

I have moved to East Sussex to a lovely little house backing onto fields and to my great joy my daughter Stephanie and her family followed, buying a house just a few miles away.

Dependent on no one, I paid for everything myself and can hold my head up high.

I have joined the Little Theatre in Lewes, where I can act, direct, and had the chance to run the Youth Drama Group.

I also use my redundant cooking skills to cater for special occasions. I feel competent and people are appreciative.

I belong to two symphony orchestras where I put my poor cello skills to the test and enjoy playing in concerts.

An art class came next to learn painting; drawing and using varied materials to make immortal works of art! Well, I am learning.

Not content with that, I became a masseur in the Alexandra Hospital for Children in Brighton, as well as working in an osteopathic clinic in Lewes.

Illnesses—I have few but have developed some nasty conditions that I try to ignore. The treatments for my ulcerative colitis with heavy-duty steroids gave me severe Osteoporosis and subsequently bronchiectasis, which can be a little inconvenient at times. However, nothing stops me from going anywhere, travelling anywhere or doing anything that I want to do. I do however have to laugh when I go to bed, wearing my sexy negligee, thinking I am a real sex kitten, only to find that not only do I have a stoma bag, but also a tube to help my breathing—surely a real turn off for even the most ardent of lovers!

My flying days in my dreams seem to be over, as I am more land bound, but can jump over great distances instead. I am also haunted by turbulent, dark water, rushing through muddy streams or murky seas which try and suck me under—but there are bright, sunny days too when I glide as if on skis over hills and over dales. I still visit beautiful places, cities, seaside bays and historic castles in my dreams that in real life have never seen.

Sometimes the dreams are frightening and sometimes Charles and my mother haunt my sleep.

Looking again back at my life, I find that I miss Germany and all I had enjoyed as a child. Thus, when I discovered an enchanting little village in the Berchtesgadener Land and a delightful, small flat nestling under the eves of a typical Bavarian house, I immediately bought it.

It is in a most beautiful part called Schonau with an immediate outlook onto Hitler's Eagles Nest, towering majestically above it. The mountain range is truly magnificent and looks different in every type of weather—sometimes sunny, sometimes threatening and sometimes just basking in a golden sunset.

The forests are large and cool, with bubbling, sparkling brooks—most inviting on hot days.

In winter skiing is abundant and great fun.

I shall look down from wherever we all end up, and enjoy seeing my legacy being enjoyed by endless generations.

Life has changed.

My grandchildren keep me young as we jump into puddles, splashing water everywhere, or kick up a storm in the autumn and laugh at the colourful leaves cascading around us like many beautiful butterflies, as they fly up into the air.

We also watch films together, while cowering behind the settee when frightened, crying when the films are sad and giggling and laughing with pure joy during the funny scenes.

I may be getting on in years, but I still feel uncertainties, hopes for the future and day dreams of magic yet to come!

They say one is as young as the young man one feels—so I embrace them all and am getting younger by the minute!

I do miss having a real soul mate with whom I can share my thoughts, my emotions, my dreams and laughter.

As we live in such a multi-racial society, I no longer worry about my foreign origin. At last I fit in, never mind where my roots came from. I am now able to enjoy foreign food, and I no longer have to worry about my continental tastes.

I count myself lucky to be cosmopolitan.

I am me—a mixture of 'sugar and spice and all things nice'.

Other people have said to me, and I quote 'that I am an exceptional and extraordinary lady, with a heart as large as the sun and a personality to go with it.' I like that and will try to live up to it.

A German song springs to mind:

Buy yourself a coloured balloon,

Hold the string tightly in your hand and you will surely be transported right into the heart of story land.

Epilogue

Looking back over my life, I still ask myself the question *'Who is Daisy? Who is Margarita?'*

The little unwanted Daisy who asked for nothing more than to be loved, and had to change into Margarita, the chameleon, who fitted into every part she had to play, be it the care free Bavarian girl, the member of the Hitler Youth, the Czech, the Catholic, the Jewish teenager, the Stateless foreigner who became Cinderella, and eventually achieved her dream of marrying the most handsome of princes.

Or is she a true Sybil an independent, divorced woman who, whatever life throws at her, faces it square on and does battle?

Countless times my persona has been torn away and my emerging personality cleaved in two. Yet I survived and emerged stronger and even more ambitious than before. My will power or perhaps my sheer stubbornness has never deserted me.

I may have received outrageous buffeting as I entered married life, but feel that much has been successful so that I may justly feel proud of what I have achieved.

In my professional life too, honours were heaped on me and all my striving was worthwhile.

Yes, mistakes were made, but they were quite unintentional. I can't blame my challenging background. I made choices and took responsibilities for them. I can't and to some degree don't want to change the past, but now that I am older, can learn from it.

Discovering the real Daisy is and what she represents is a never-ending exploration. There is still so much to do, to learn and to accomplish. I have by no means finished with life and neither has life finished with me. I will continue unabated, for the real Daisy to find herself, and as all good stories go, live happily ever after.

Printed in Great Britain
by Amazon.co.uk, Ltd.,
Marston Gate.